Curtains
& Blinds

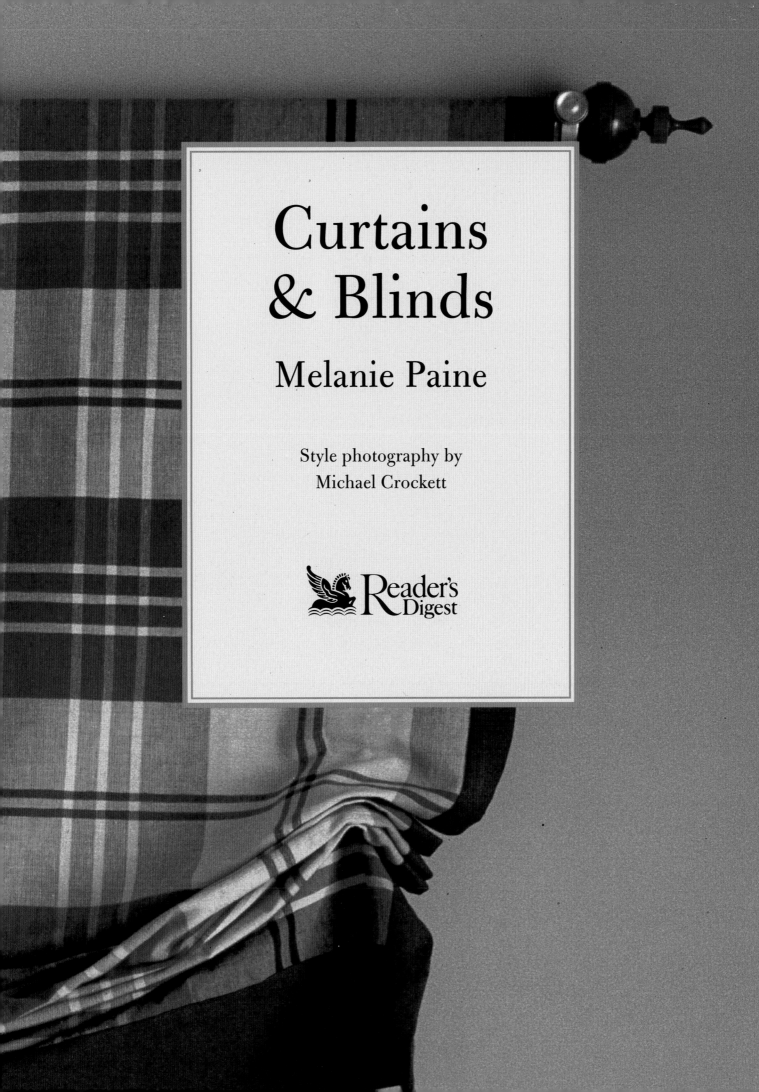

Curtains & Blinds

Melanie Paine

Style photography by
Michael Crockett

Reader's Digest

A READER'S DIGEST BOOK

Published by
The Reader's Digest Association Limited
11 Westferry Circus
Canary Wharf
London E14 4HE

1 3 5 7 9 8 6 4 2

British Library Cataloguing-in-Publication Data:
A catalogue record for this title is available from the British Library.

ISBN 0 276 42327 5

Conceived, edited and designed by
Collins & Brown Limited

Editorial Director: Colin Ziegler
Editor: Jinny Johnson
Art Director: Roger Bristow
Designer: Sarah Davies
Style photography by Michael Crockett
Styling by Melanie Paine
Sets built by Steve Gott
Step-by-step photography by Sampson Lloyd and Geoff Dann
Illustrations by Ian Sidaway

Colour separation by Daylight Colour Art, Singapore
Printed by New Interlitho SpA, Italy

CONTENTS

The Basic Techniques

The Projects

INTRODUCTION

IMAGINATIVE WINDOW FURNISHINGS can transform your home. The right style of curtain or blind is the quickest, simplest way of softening a stark interior, concealing an unpleasant view or bringing new brightness and colour to a room. Depending on your choice of fabric, curtains or blinds can make a room look warm and cosy or create a cool, refreshing ambiance. A curtain may be as simple as a sheer fabric threaded on a pole slot-head style or a more ornate arrangement in luxurious velvet with a contrasting gathered drape. A plain Roman blind lends a classic subtlety while a more complex pleated blind becomes a focal point.

When you start making your own curtains and blinds you will find that there is a vast and ever-changing array of fabrics available to inspire you. I find that keeping a collection of swatches is an ideal way of learning about fabrics. Look at as many varieties of colour, pattern, texture and weight as possible to help you appreciate what fabrics can and cannot do. Some, such as wool damask, drape particularly well and suggest gracious floor-length curtains, falling in soft folds. Crisp cottons hold their shape and are ideal for stylish shades. Don't be afraid to combine different types of fabric in one arrangement – in the right situation, opposites, such as velvet and silk taffeta, look wonderful. There are few hard and fast rules other than to keep a balance.

A window is not simply an arrangement of glass and timber. It frames your view of the outside world. It lets in light and contributes a great deal to the character of a room. Proportion plays an important part in styling windows, and it is best to be guided by what is there rather than trying to distort it. Before you begin to make curtains or blinds, assess the shape of your window and decide on the best approach. Then turn to the pages on choosing a style and browse through the array of types of support, headings and fabrics to help you select what is right for your home. Decide if you want to have a chunky pole with decorative finials or a more discreet concealed support; look at the wide range of headings to chose from, and consider using embellishments such as fringes and tiebacks.

The basic skills of making curtains and blinds are explained in the chapter on basic techniques, from how to measure your window and estimate how much fabric to buy, to how to put up a pole and make a hand-pleated heading. This section provides all the back-up information you need as you work through the projects.

The projects cover a range of curtain and blind styles from the very simple to the more ornate, each featuring a different technique. Clear step-by-step instructions guide you through the process of making these beautiful window furnishings and cross references to the basic techniques help you find all the help you need.

I hope that the projects and the other ideas that I have included in this book encourage you to make your own innovative and professional-looking curtains and blinds. Once you start, you will be amazed at how easy it is to transform your windows. Be inspired and start sewing!

Melanie Paine 1997

ASSESSING WINDOWS

WINDOWS function as providers of light, as architectural detail and as frames through which you view the outside world. They are important features in a room and you should take into account their various functions when choosing how to dress them. Therefore, before deciding on a style of curtain or blind, first consider the shape and proportions of your window in relation to the rest of the room and whether its position in the room poses any limitations on the type of window treatments you can use.

Most windows fall into one of these categories: portrait (taller than wide), landscape (wider than high) or square. There can of course be multiples of these and in some cases two or more portrait windows that are side by side in a wall may become a landscape shape. Portrait windows are the most common shape and the most versatile in

Pair of identical windows in same wall

These should be treated as one or in the same way. You could opt for two pairs of curtains, two blinds or one single curtain on each window, mirroring one another (see p. 86).

Two different windows in same wall

Whether you use curtains or blinds, give smaller, lower height windows a heading at the same level as their larger neighbour. Consider the decorative impact when curtains are open and windows revealed, as well as when they are closed.

Two or more different windows in the same room

In this situation it pays to choose different arrangements for the different window styles, but to stick to the same fabrics. If, for example, one pair of curtains has a contrast border, then use the same idea on a neighbouring blind. You can also link the two by using the same style poles or tiebacks.

Window or sliding door taking up all or most of a wall

Here, you need to think carefully about where the curtains will hang when the window or door is open. Often there is little room to either side of the window, therefore avoid thick fabrics or heavily gathered headings that will cause the fabric to bulk.

French windows

These lend themselves to a pair of curtains hanging down both sides. There may be some restrictions if the doors open inwards so position poles wisely. Keep curtaining simple and hold curtains off the windows with tiebacks to provide clear access.

Bay window

The normal way to treat a bay window is with a curved track concealed with some kind of pelmet or fascia (see p. 76). However, you could treat each window singly, with Roman or panel blinds, for example.

terms of how they can be dressed. They are often set high in the wall and can extend to the floor as with French windows (see opposite). Portrait windows can take a pair of curtains in any style, most forms of blind or a single curtain, perhaps extended to the floor to accentuate the shape and held with a tieback on one side.

Landscape windows range from large picture windows and sliding doors to side-by-side loft windows and small casements. Pairs of curtains in most styles suit this category. However, keep your headings relatively simple to

avoid making the window appear squat and top heavy. Where windows are very wide, curtaining can be difficult as there is so much fabric to 'store' at each side. Consider blinds for a simpler, less cluttered feel.

Square windows can be tiny cottage windows, often recessed, or much larger windows that are often found in more contemporary homes. For the former you need a treatment that does not need much space around the window, while for the latter you need one that lets in the maximum light during the day.

Single window in a wall
Here, you have almost carte blanche. Whichever style you choose, remain close to the proportions of the window. Instead of a pair of curtains, you could balance a single curtain with furniture or pictures or hang a blind.

Window close to an adjacent wall
This often results from a room being partitioned leaving a window off-centre. Emphasize this asymmetry and go for a single curtain with a strongly decorative headings and chunky tieback (see p. 64).

Window close to a ceiling
If there is no wall space for a support, you can use a ceiling fixing, or fix a fabric-covered board securely to the ceiling to spread the weight of a pole or track beneath it.

Window in a deep recess
This requires simple window furnishings – slot-head curtains on slim poles or those that can swing out from their fixings. If light is important, avoid bulky fabrics that will block the window. Fix poles close to the window and into the frame.

Window with radiator beneath
This problem is best treated with a simple design solution such as a sill-length curtain or blind. Or, ignore the radiator and go for floor-length curtains. Try, for example, a single curtain on a pole pulled back to one side and balanced with a chunky rope looped around the curtainless end of the pole.

Window on stairs, where floor is uneven
Blinds are ideal for this situation, but you could consider a single curtain, embellished with wonderful tiebacks or ornate finials.

Choosing a Style

ELEMENTS OF STYLE

WITH CURTAINS AND BLINDS, there are a number of different elements that combine together to influence the overall look, and you can use each one to add style and interest to your window treatment.

The most important element is the fabric you choose, whether it be a delicate muslin or voile for a light and airy effect, rich and inviting velvet or tapestry for a warm, sumptuous feel or boldly patterned and brightly coloured fabric for a look that will dominate a room. Consider the texture and weight of the fabric as well as its colour and pattern and decide whether you want the curtain or blind to blend in with the rest of the decoration or to stand out as a feature.

The support you choose will also influence the finished look of your curtain or, to a lesser extent, blind. First decide whether you want wall, window frame or ceiling attachments. Curtain poles come in many different styles and are often a decorative feature in their own right, especially when you combine them with rings and finials. Alternatively, use track, either left uncovered or hidden with a lath and fascia, a pelmet or a drape hung from a pole above. With certain types of blind you can use a pole, but generally a blind is attached to a lath.

A separate, but closely linked element, is your choice of heading. This controls the way your curtains hang so use the heading positively to reinforce the style you have chosen. If you want a simple effect, with the fabric falling as a flat panel when the curtain is pulled across, try a slot heading around a pole or a series of hand-sewn hooks attached to rings. Alternatively, for a richer effect, gather the curtains with tape for extra fullness or sew them up into more elaborate pleats. This will make a special feature of the heading and allow the fabric to drape and fold in different ways all the way down its length. Although the fabric of most blinds falls as a flat panel from the lath or pole, you can introduce pleats that run from top to bottom and are accentuated when the blind is pulled up.

Finally, you can further influence the style of your windows by adding embellishments. Combine their practical purposes – tiebacks that keep curtains off the window or ties that hold up simple panel blinds – with their decorative potential. Embellishments add texture and definition to your window treatment – from simple piping to contrast border panels and fringing.

You can use all these different elements to influence the overall design and add a personalized touch to your decor. Try making some unexpected combinations such as complementing a grand fabric with a simple wooden pole and hand-sewn hooks, or a simple fabric with a grand goblet pleat heading and braid border, while holding it off the window with a tasselled tieback. Also remember that there is a degree of interdependence between the different elements; your choice of fabric will be limited by the maximum weight that the support can take, while the way a fabric hangs and the type of pattern it has should influence the type of heading you choose.

SUPPORT

When choosing your support (see pp. 14–17), consider both its aesthetic appeal and the characteristics of the window. Look at the amount of space available for attaching a support, as well as the weight of the fabric it must hold.

HEADING

Headings (see pp. 18–19) provide decoration at the top of your curtain or blind and control how the fabric hangs down its length. You can use them to emphasise a grand design or give an extra touch to a simple curtain.

An unusual solution

This treatment demonstrates how the different elements of style work together. In this unusual situation, curtains are hung halfway up huge windows. The simple wire support is almost invisible, leaving the view through the windows unimpeded when the curtains are pulled back. The heading – a row of eyelets punched along the top of the curtain – is in keeping with the support, and the curtains are, by necessity, unlined and made of a light fabric so that the wire can support them.

FABRIC

The type of fabric (see pp. 20–27) does most to influence the look. Whether you choose heavy or light, warm or cool, or subtle or striking fabrics, make sure that your choice of heading suits your choice of fabric and that the support is strong enough to hold its weight.

EMBELLISHMENT

Use embellishments – ties, tassels, braid, fringing (see pp. 28–31) – both for practical purposes, such as holding back a curtain, or holding up a blind, and for adding extra texture and definition to the edges of your window treatment.

CHOOSING A SUPPORT

OR CURTAINS, poles are the most attractive kind of support (see pp. 16–17 for details on the many varieties of poles and their accessories). They are attached to the wall, window frame or the ceiling with brackets (see p. 52). The curtain is supported on rings and, as both pole and rings are visible, they can contribute greatly to the overall style of your window treatment.

The other option is to use track, which is functional rather than decorative. It can be left uncovered but is more often concealed, the simplest method being with lath and fascia covered with fabric. The lath is a piece of wood fitted at right angles to the wall or window frame and supported by an angle bracket. The fascia, a slim piece of plywood, is fixed to its front to hide the track.

POLE

The simplest types of poles rest in an architrave bracket that is fixed to a wall. Small screws at the front of the bracket are screwed into the pole once it is in place to secure it (see p. 52 for instructions on putting up a pole).

Wall screw • Pole • Screw into pole at front of bracket • Wall • Brass architrave bracket

UNCOVERED TRACK

Tracks are available in plastic and metal, but metal is better because it is stronger. For best results, order track from a professional who can also install it, especially if it needs to be curved. If you do it yourself, follow instructions provided with the track, since they vary from brand to brand (see also p. 53).

Wall screw • Track • Wall • Hole for curtain hook in glider • Curtain hook • Bracket attaching track to wall

Ceiling-fitted pole
This brass pole supports a straightforward curtain arrangement. The pole is suspended from long brackets fitted on chunky ceiling beams. It is always easier to fit pole brackets into wood rather than walls and a ceiling fixing is sometimes the answer.

Invisible track
Tracks are generally covered, but in some situations a simple thin white metal or plastic track 'disappears' against a window frame or into the top of a recess. In this example, the track is hardly visible and does not detract from the curtains' look.

Some tracks are already corded when purchased. This is especially good if you intend to hang light-coloured or delicate fabrics because the curtains do not have to be handled when pulled across the window. You can use them when there is not enough room between window and ceiling for a pole and you can bend them to fit the angles of a bay or the curves of a bow window. This is not easy, however, and it is best done by a professional.

Whether you use a pole or track, remember that heavy or full-length curtains always need substantial support and that any installation is only as strong as the surface to which it is attached. If a wall is too soft or uneven, brackets should be fitted into the window frame, which is likely to be stronger. Avoid using ceiling tracks unless there are wooden beams that can support the brackets.

Your choice of support for blinds is far simpler. You can hang some styles of blind from a pole if they have a slot heading or attach them with café clips (see p. 17). But, generally, blinds are hung from a lath attached to the wall with brackets. If there is no room for the brackets, or if you want to hang a blind in front of a recess, you can attach the lath to the ceiling with a screw.

COVERED TRACK

You can hide track with a lath and fascia. The lath – a 5- x 2.5-cm (2- x 1-in) piece of wood – is fitted at right angles to the wall and the fascia – a slim piece of plywood – fixed to its front (see pp. 56–57 for how to put up laths). The track is fixed to the lath's underside and the fascia is deep enough to hide the track, while allowing the runners to move freely.

LATH FOR BLIND

A wooden lath to support a blind is fixed to the ceiling with screws or supported on angle brackets that are screwed to the wall. The lath itself is covered in fabric to match the blind, making a discreet fixing (see pp. 55–57 for instructions on covering and securing laths).

Using a lath and fascia
The track that supports these curtains is hidden by a lath and fascia covered in the same fabric as the curtains. A track was a good choice here since there is little space above the doors to fit a pole.

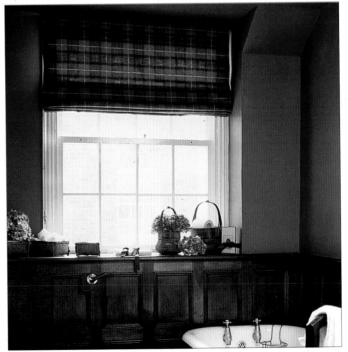

Blind on a lath
One of the advantages of using a lath is that it is hidden. The blind appears simply as a panel of fabric unencumbered by brackets and poles. In this example, the lath is supported by angle brackets that are attached to the window frame.

Poles and accessories

Wrought iron rod and finial in one

Chrome rod with matching finial

Dark wood pole with matching finial

Painted wood pole with matching finial

Thick brass pole with decorative finial

Thin brass pole with fleur-de-lys finial

Poles come in a wide range of materials and finishes, including polished or painted wood, brushed nickel, antique brass or wrought iron. They can be fun or formal, handmade or mass-produced, carved and gilded or even pasted in wallpaper.

Poles are supported on chunky wooden brackets or on slender brass versions. For poles that have to be fitted into a recess or against an adjacent wall there are special brackets that encase the end of the pole. These are available in wood or brass to match the pole.

Finials are the ornaments fitted onto each end of the pole, to one end if the pole abuts a wall. They perform the practical task of stopping the last curtain ring from falling

Poles

Give as much thought to choosing the style of pole and finial as to the curtain or blind itself. Try mixing brass and wood together or contrasting different colours of wood. If you are using a beautiful pole, make sure that the style of curtain allows it to be seen to full advantage.

Finials

Many poles come with matching finials and some have finials that are actually a part of the pole. Others can be fitted to any pole and give you a chance to experiment with different combinations. Try teaming an ornate pole with simple finials or dress up a plain pole with the wildest finials you can find.

RINGS

Brass ring   **Wooden ring**   **Iron ring**   **Painted ring**

off the rod, but they are also decorative elements in their own right and often provide a much needed finishing touch to a window treatment.

Attaching your curtain or blind

Rings are the most common form of attachment for curtains and most poles come with matching rings. Despite this, experiment with different combinations of pole and ring if you feel so inclined – just remember that the rings need to be at least 1.25 cm (½ in) larger in diameter than the pole.

As an alternative to rings, chrome or brass eyelets punched through the top of the curtain make a strong decorative device. Tapes, ribbon ties or fabric tabs sewn at intervals across the top of a curtain also look pretty, either in the same fabric as the main curtain or in a contrasting colour or pattern. In the case of fabric tabs, loop them over the pole and fasten them to the curtain with a button or stud.

You can stitch a slot at the top of your curtain or blind and then simply thread a pole into it. The pole is then hidden, apart from the finials at either end.

A similar option is to use clips that grip the top of the curtain or blind and encircle the pole. They are available in a variety of finishes from brass or bronze to painted metal. If you choose to create a slot or use clips for curtains, remember that you will not be able to draw them back. For this reason, they generally work best with lightweight fabrics that do not block out all of the daylight.

Twisted wire
These interestingly shaped pieces of wire act as both rings and hooks. They are set off by the simplicity of the bare metal pole and eyelet heading.

OTHER ATTACHMENTS

Eyelet and rope **Tie** **Tab and button** **Café clip**

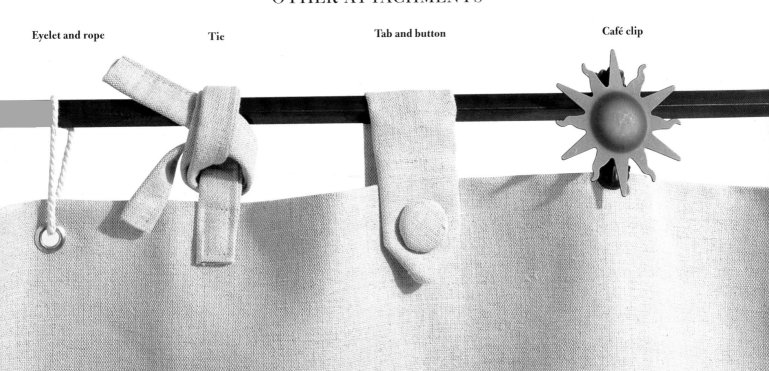

CHOOSING A HEADING

THE HEADING RUNS horizontally across the top of the window treatment and controls the way the fabric hangs. With curtains, there is normally some fullness in their width – more fabric than window width – and how the fabric is pulled up into the finished width is determined by the type of heading used.

At its most basic, the heading can make the fabric hang as a flat panel with hardly any fullness. You can achieve this with a slot heading or by sewing hooks or ties on to the curtain and attaching it to rings on a pole.

For a gathered heading you sew special curtain tape to the top of the curtain at the back when it is flat. Strings

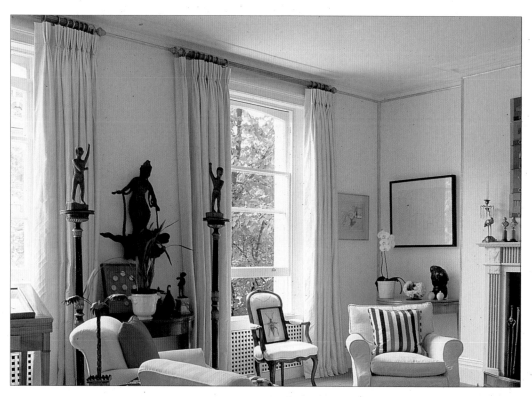

Formal pleats
Smart, cream-coloured curtains with a French, or pinch, pleat heading are ideal for this simple, yet sophisticated room. The groups of pleats, spaced at regular intervals across the top of the curtain, hold the fabric in neatly disciplined folds. They can be used with tracks or poles.

Slot heading
Simple to make (see p. 48), this works best for blinds and short, lightweight curtains that don't need to be pulled across.

Goblet pleats
An impressive formal heading (see p. 51), this is good for long curtains and is often used with rich, heavy fabrics.

Gathered heading
Use 2.5-cm (1-in) tape for a simple gathered heading (see p. 49). It is suitable for both small, casual curtains and long, full curtains.

Box pleats
Box pleats provide a neat, structured look (see p. 51). They work particularly well with crisp, thin fabrics as opposed to bulkier ones.

that run through the tape are then pulled until the curtain is reduced to the required width. The two most common tapes are 2.5-cm (1-in) tape, which gives a simple gathered heading and is usually set down from the top of the curtain to make a 'stand up' heading above the tape, and 7.5-cm (3-in) tape, which gives deep pencil pleats, producing multiple folds in the fabric.

There are also tapes available for making French, box and even goblet pleats, but it is better if you do these by hand since they will look and hang much better. This is especially true when you are hanging your curtain from a pole since the heading will be visible.

When choosing your curtain heading, make sure that it is suitable for the fabrics and appropriate for the setting. Bleached canvas on the windows of a loft conversion would look odd arranged in neat French pleats. A heavy classical brocade would not work with a narrow slot heading. But don't be afraid to experiment and arrive at unpredictable combinations. Shot taffeta silk could look splendid with a heading of chunky eyelets, or rich velvet curtains with brightly coloured tab headings.

For blinds, there is not the same degree of choice as with curtains. Whether a pole or lath is used to support the blind, the fabric simply hangs down from the top like a flat panel. Any folds or pleats in a blind do not rely so much on the heading as on the way in which the blind is raised. Depending on the type of cording system used (see p. 54), the blind will bunch or fold in different ways when it is pulled up, and some will form delicate scooped shapes along the bottom.

Simple slot heading

Two parallel lines of stitching through doubled fabric at the top of this curtain make a simple sleeve, or slot, through which the pole is threaded. Slot-headed curtains can only be partially opened. When closed, the fabric can fall as a flat panel or, if the curtain has more fullness as shown here, take on a gathered appearance.

Pencil pleats
Created with 7.5-cm (3-in) tape, the fabric is gathered into tight pleats (see p. 48). This heading is best used beneath pelmets or drapes.

Hand-sewn hooks
These hooks (see p. 49) work with most fabrics and give a simple, ungathered look. They can be visible as here, or hidden behind the top of the curtain or blind.

French pleats
A formal heading, this is made of groups of three pleats (see p. 50). The style is most suitable for long, floor-length curtains.

Eyelets
Easy to make with a punch and dye kit (see p. 49), eyelets create an attractive, informal effect on curtains or blinds.

CHOOSING A FABRIC

Light or heavy

THE COLOUR AND TEXTURE of a fabric determines its style and the effect it has on a room. Light fabrics may look frivolous, while heavy fabrics may appear more serious and grand. A richly patterned tapestry, for example, is weighty and usually comes in traditional dark colours. Curtains in such a fabric would rightly dominate a room, and accessories as well as other furnishings should be of equal stature. At the other end of the scale, fine, beautiful pale silks or linens lend an airiness that the rest of the room should follow. Pale, neutral colours on walls and other furnishings would extend the feeling of lightness. But equally, a rich dark red wall would accentuate the fragility and beauty of such light fabrics.

Woven fabrics, particularly those with textured embellishments, such as brocade, are among some of the heaviest. Wool, which is one of the heaviest fibres, produces some of the heaviest fabrics. But cotton, too, can be heavy if the weave structure is dense. Flimsy, loosely woven cottons, such as lace or muslin, however, are feather-light. Silk is generally finely woven and makes a light fabric. Heavy, richly textured fabrics, such as tapestry and damask, need to be anchored with strong fabrics on cushions or throws and should be appropriate to the

Light and airy
Graceful folds of white muslin cover the whole of this ceiling-to-floor and wall-to-wall window. The curtains protect the room from the direct rays of the sun, yet still allow it to be bathed in light, giving an airy feel.

LIGHT FABRICS

The delicate floral pattern on this cotton fabric gives it a gentle appearance.

The ground colour of this cotton stripe lightens its appearance. It would work both on its own and as a lining for heavier fabrics.

A painted silver pattern swirls across the surface of this cotton fabric, giving it a light, graceful look.

A delicate lacy fabric with a leaf motif, this has an open weave that allows light to shine through.

The pale background pattern adds a subtle lightness to this cotton floral print.

overall decor of the room. Use chunky wooden or painted finials or old brass pelmets as embellishments and add heavy tassels or fringes to edges. Heavy fabrics need sturdy support, so make sure that the wall or window frame is strong enough to hold a weighty pole or track.

Points to note

• Sheer and open-weave fabrics, such as muslin and lace, allow plenty of light into a room and protect other furnishings from direct sunlight. Use sheers on their own on a window or with heavier main curtains or blinds.

• Lace is often made in a panel with one central design and side borders. To look their best, these panels should be hung, without fullness, from a slim pole or rod. For an attractive, light-diffusing effect, back open-weave fabrics, such as lace and voile, with a coloured lining.

• A heavy fabric is warmer, excludes light and keeps out drafts. Some heavy fabrics, such as tapestry and thick wool chenille, are bulky and their weave makes them stiff. These fabrics are wonderful for panel blinds that roll up or for flatter styles of curtain. They do not drape or pleat easily, so do not use them for curtains with headings that rely on tight pleating or neat folds. Velvet, on the other hand, is fluid despite its thickness and works well with pleated headings.

Heavy and opulent

The weighty fabrics used for these curtains and blind combine to give a look of warmth and sumptuousness. They are ideal for a bedroom as they would block out even the brightest dawn and provide a cosy atmosphere on cold winter nights.

HEAVY FABRICS

A heavy tapestry fabric woven as a 30-cm (12-in) strip works well as an edging for plain fabrics.

The ribbed surface of this patterned and striped cotton adds stiffness. It can be used for borders or for curtains or blinds.

This rich brocade in traditional colours drapes beautifully, despite its weight, and makes excellent curtains.

The surface on this thick, gold-patterned wool is slightly raised. The fabric is reversible.

A dramatic weighty silk damask, this needs to be used on a large-scale to show its pattern to full effect.

Plain or patterned

Both plain and patterned fabrics come in a wide variety of styles. With plain fabrics, texture is all important since there is no pattern or mix of colours to obscure it. Think of velvet, hessian, silk or roughly textured cotton – each has its own particular surface that gives it character and alters the way light interacts with the cloth. Natural fabrics, such as cotton, give a simple, fresh look; wool and velvet bring warmth to a room and can also add a degree of grandeur; while silk possesses a refined, elegant quality.

With pattern, it is the design and the scale of the design that sets the tone. Floral motifs add an informal, country touch to a room, while a bold stripe always introduces a sense of elegant classicism.

Harmony and contrast

When choosing your fabric always consider the other decoration in the room first. Plain fabrics can work well with plain coloured walls and floors to create a minimalist look. But if you find a lack of contrast monotonous, you could add a patterned wall or break it up with pictures.

When using patterned fabrics the key is always to achieve the right balance. Use patterned fabric with plain and make the colours harmonize or contrast, depending on the visual effect you want to achieve. A dark brown border will soften the effect of a dazzling black and white patterned curtain. You can even mix pattern with pattern, provided that there is a strong colour link between the two – an edging in a busy floral print, for example, adds pattern to a strong stripe. When mixing patterns it is crucial to make it clear where one begins and another ends or the result is likely to be a muddled mess.

Natural simplicity
Bleached cream surfaces harmonize beneath a flood of natural light to create an atmosphere of simplicity and calm in this elegant interior. The stark geometry of the window panes is offset by the plain, neutral fabrics used for the furniture and blinds. The effect is one of light and shadow, shape and form.

PLAIN FABRICS

This robust red cotton twill is plain, in that it is all one colour, but strongly textured. It drapes very well.

More matt than gloss, the surface of this plain green velvet catches just enough light to give it richness.

A woven motif, with raised and flat areas, creates an overall pattern so subtle that the fabric appears plain.

This chenille has a tiny gold motif, which gives it character. It drapes beautifully and makes good borders.

From a distance, this fabric appears to be plain and all one colour, but the tiny check adds interest close up.

Points to note

• When using plain or subtly patterned fabrics, you need to consider carefully the properties of the fabric that you choose. As there is no pattern to distract the eye, the texture of the fabric and the way that it folds and hangs becomes crucial.

• When using plain fabric on a large window, avoid using primary or near primary colours – a broad expanse of just one colour might be overpowering.

• Do not use fabric with a large pattern on a small window since there will not be enough space to see the whole design. Conversely, if you use a fabric with a small pattern on a large window, be aware that from a distance the pattern disappears and the fabric appears as one colour.

• Choose your heading with care when using patterned fabrics; elaborate pleats could obscure the pattern. As a general rule, the more ornate the pattern, the simpler the heading should be.

Casual gingham

The relaxed country style of this kitchen is complemented by the classically simple blue and white check used for these curtains. For added harmony, the same fabric was used for the cushion on the chair.

PATTERNED FABRICS

A variation on the French toile de Jouy, this is a beautifully printed pattern with many soft colours.

This striking motif, on a thick, heavy cotton fabric, would stand out in any decorating scheme.

A dramatic fabric with architectural motifs, this is best used flat to give the pattern its full impact.

With its lively overall pattern, this chintz can be used flat or gathered into curtains. It drapes well.

Classic club stripes add a touch of distinction to any room. Woven in wool, this rich fabric has a subtle line of yellow.

Warm or cool

Colour is the most important factor in determining whether a fabric looks warm or cool. There are of course 'warm' blues and 'cool' reds, but a blue and white stripe will generally look and feel cooler than a red and white stripe. However, texture also plays a part. Some blues look warmer in a woven matt fabric, while a glazed fabric can appear cool even when in a bright colour.

Earthy colours, such as ochre, terracotta, olive green and burgundy give a feeling of warmth and cosiness. Easy on the eye, they are undemanding in terms of other furnishings and decoration. Acid yellows and sharp greens are cooler and more dominant. They need careful balancing and are best used in a quality cloth.

Colour combinations

Colours, when combined, affect one another. A stripe of navy blue will cool a vibrant scarlet curtain, but add turquoise or cobalt blue instead, and the scarlet becomes even more dramatic. Strong lime green and indigo are both cool colours but can look hot if used together – despite the old adage 'blue and green should never be seen'.

When combining colours, balance is the key to success. Flamboyant colour combinations can look stunning but they need careful consideration or they may become a confusing muddle. Use strident colours in smaller areas

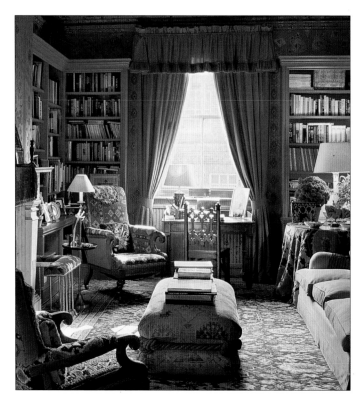

Warm exuberance
Warmth and richness exude from every surface in this beautifully decorated interior. Intense reds, golds and warm ochres dominate and, although they are balanced by the cooler colours in the carpet, create an exuberant atmosphere. The red of the dramatic curtain arrangement, which is definitely at the hot end of the colour spectrum, is intensified by the natural light streaming through the window.

WARM FABRICS

Ochre and terracotta, both warm earthy colours, combine in this woven ribbed cotton.

A pale coffee-coloured background softens the rich reds and yellows in this exuberantly designed chintz.

A deep rust-red background gives this Paisley patterned cotton print a warm look.

Rich colours and a soft texture combine to give a warm feel to this woven brocade.

The buttercup yellow of this woollen damask creates a warm sunny glow.

for the best effect. A bright panel of warm primary colour on a curtain or blind hung in a room decorated in black and white would be dramatic.

Try making interesting pairs of colours – warm yellow with cool navy; pale coffee with rich burgundy. Colour can also allow you to link different fabrics. A rich heavy velvet can work well with a shiny checked taffeta if there is a colour in common. Even the tiniest thread of colour can join two or more completely different fabrics into a workable partnership.

Try making a scrapbook of samples of different types of fabrics; it will help you to create unexpected and interesting combinations. Remember, though, that colours that look wonderful on a small scale might not work well when spread over a large area.

Points to note

- If sharp white laces and linens appear too cool, soften the effect with honey-coloured jute tiebacks and a rich red mahogany pole.
- Warm up cool dark rooms with an array of fiery colours that reflect light and add zing.
- Some colours, such as citrus lime and lemon, can be hot or cool. The colours in the rest of the room affect how they appear in any decorative situation.
- Fabrics influence the surfaces that surround them. Crisp white cotton with whitewashed walls and a stone floor make a room look and feel cool. If a cream fabric is used instead of brilliant white, the rest of the room will be subtly warmed.
- Fabrics are affected by the light in a room. Natural light and electric light change the way a fabric looks so bear this in mind when making your choice.

Cool checks
Sparklingly fresh, this crisp blue and white fabric sweeps across bright bay windows, keeping out the sun and lowering the temperature. A plain blue border at the top continues the cool theme and helps to define the shape of the window.

COOL FABRICS

This cool, crisp poplin drapes beautifully and also looks good as a pleated or rolled blind.

A classic blue and white plaid, this cotton check can be used for any type of curtain, blind or border.

These blue tulips printed on silk would be best shown off on floor-length curtains with a simple gathered heading.

This inky-blue velvet drapes in thick folds and is excellent for heavy curtains.

A crisp cotton with a cool blue and red pattern, this works well for flat curtains or pleated blinds.

Subtle or striking

Subtle fabrics, with their quiet elegance, usually blend comfortably with their surroundings. Using fabrics with subtle patterns or colours, however, requires careful thought. A mix of whites, off-whites and pale coffee fabrics in one curtain arrangement could look lovely, provided the rest of the decor is also subtle and does not distract. White on white, or close to white, patterns look handsome and can be combined with other subtle fabrics. For example,

try making a blind in white cotton with a small motif in cream, border it with a pale coffee and white stripe and hang it from a scrubbed white pole. Minimal colour combinations in interesting textures can produce restful, but beautiful results.

Other fabrics, which truly dazzle and shock, can offer a room dramatic charm. Imagine a single window with a flourish of pink velvet around its frame in a white room

Subtle serenity
Balance and symmetry, achieved by a quiet but clever use of colour and form, are the key elements in this interior. The window furnishings blend with the walls. The blinds are functional but do not make a strong decorative statement. Instead they are a subtle part of the room's architecture.

SUBTLE FABRICS

Muted greys and blues combine with a red and ochre plaid in this soft woollen tweed.

This lightweight sheer cotton fabric has a barely visible thin stripe woven through it.

A small square motif gives this heavy white cotton fabric subtle pattern and texture.

The two colours in this woven fabric are very close in tone, giving the impression of subtle pattern.

This classic black and cream ticking is in a soft cotton that drapes well.

with stripped floor boards. The setting allows such a striking fabric to stand out and calls attention to its drama.

Many striking fabrics have bold colour combinations – bright orange against aquamarine with a dash of raspberry pink, for example. Use this kind of fabric for a plain blind or for a curtain with a simple heading of hand-sewn hooks or clips. Contrasting surfaces and texture, as well as colour can also present striking combinations within a blind or set of curtains. Try using shiny, bright fabrics alongside those with a matt surface.

Points to note

• A strong colour or dramatic pattern can be balanced by a more soothing, subtle palette. One should attractively enhance the other, but avoid too obvious clashes where the combination of subtle touches and drama is overdone.

• Avoid using large, striking designs on small windows as the intended dramatic effect may be lost.

• When planning to decorate a room with dramatic fabrics whose image or pattern could be dominant, try to select from large fabric samples. Hold them up at the window, if possible, so that their colour or pattern or both may be read from a distance. Often what you see on a tiny scrap of fabric changes completely when scaled up.

• When working on adjacent rooms, the decoration and furnishing should be considered together. This is especially so with rooms that open off halls or landings for example, where the relationship between subtle or striking is paramount.

• To achieve a dramatic effect you need to be able to see and 'read' the fabric clearly. Striking fabrics have the strength to stand on their own. They do not need complicated arrangements, which only lessen their effect.

• You can use a mixture of bold, strong patterns if colour links the different fabrics and the overall arrangement is kept fairly simple.

Bold tartan
The shape of this room and the position of its windows make it a challenge to curtain. This bold, predominantly red tartan is a suitably dramatic fabric and makes a wide sweep of strong colour and pattern.

STRIKING FABRICS

The boldness of this wool tartan in strident colours is its strength, and it should be used flamboyantly.

A figured velvet in rich luscious colours, this fabric shimmers as the light catches its surface.

With its striking pattern on a black ground, this heavy cotton weave needs to be used in dramatic surroundings.

An Indian cotton, woven in an unusual colour combination, would make bold curtains or blinds.

The vivid contrasting stripes of this cotton print can be used horizontally or vertically and make good flat blinds.

EMBELLISHMENTS

FRINGES, BRAIDS, TASSELS, BUTTONS and other kinds of embellishments are all ways to add interest to curtains and blinds. Purely decorative, they provide contrasting colour and texture. They are usually applied around the edges of a curtain or blind by hand and help to define its shape. The addition of a navy blue chenille fringe along the leading edge of a curtain in pale cream silk, for example, lifts the arrangement and gives the eye a line to follow when the curtain is pulled back.

There are many ways to use such embellishments. Hand-sew plain flat braids to the edges of Roman blinds before the fabric is made up. Or add flat fabric borders in contrasting fabrics or colours to the edges of curtains or blinds, again defining shape and adding additional colour or texture. These borders, sewn to the fabric before it is made up, can be on the perimeter or inset in the main fabric and be made from one piece or alternate colours. Adding borders is also a good way of mixing different textures of fabric together. Consider combining a rough hessian with a simple flat cotton, both in the same colour.

Cord or rope made from cotton or silks or a combination of both can define the edge of a curtain. Hand sewn to the finished curtain along the leading edge or across the heading, this is a subtle way of adding texture.

Row of button tufts

Key tassel

Using tassels and button tufts
You can embellish the base of a blind with a row of button tufts running along just above the bottom edge or with tassels hanging down from it. Use small chunky key tassels in cotton, wool and raffia or simple mattress tufts in dyed cotton.

Embellishing the edges of curtains
A border, piping or fringe down the edge of a curtain should look as though it belongs to the fabric it decorates. Colour should relate to the fabric or to a nearby decorative element in the room. Here, the curtain fringe tones perfectly with the silk fabric of the curtains and lends weight and texture.

Using fringes and borders

To give added definition, colour and texture to the base of a blind, you can hand-sew on a fringe. If your main fabric is neutral, try jazzing it up with a contrasting border such as a striking strip of tapestry (see above).

—EMBELLISHING THE TOP OF A CURTAIN—

Self-pelmet

To give extra interest to the heading of a curtain, add a fringe to the front so that it adorns the top of the curtain like a pelmet. You can use a completely different fabric, as shown here, but there should at least be a colour link between the two.

Soft drape

Another way of embellishing the top of a curtain is with a drape of fabric that hangs from a pole above the curtain and hides the curtain's heading. The drape pictured here, with its dark red horizontal stripe, adds a dash of bold colour to the simple calico curtain hanging beneath it.

Using tiebacks

Tiebacks are both decorative and practical. They hold the curtain back from the window to allow in as much light as possible, but they also shape the curtain into graceful folds. Generally, a tieback loops around a concealed hook fixed into the wall next to the window.

Rope and tassel tiebacks are available ready-made. Better still, make your own from a variety of different materials. Silk and lengths of tapestry fabric make beautiful tiebacks, but simple jute also looks extremely effective. Add tassels to lengths of jute or plait several lengths together. Lengths of ribbon or braid, with rings sewn at each end for looping over the hook, or tied for more casual effect, work well and are easily changed to give a new look. For full-length curtains, fix tiebacks at roughly one-third the length of the curtain from the floor. However, if you are using long tassels, place the hooks farther up so that the tassels hang correctly against the curtain.

Alternatively, you can use tiebacks that are made of wood, brass or other metal. Simply fix the tieback to the wall so that the curtain can be looped behind it, making sure that the back edge of the curtain remains vertical. This arrangement generally only works when the curtain hangs just past each side of the window and the tieback is fitted close to the frame or window edge. Rosettes, in brass or wood, may also be used as glorified hooks for holding rope tiebacks.

You cannot use a tieback with blinds, but in much the same way as you use a tieback to hold back a curtain, you can use a tie to hold up a simple panel blind.

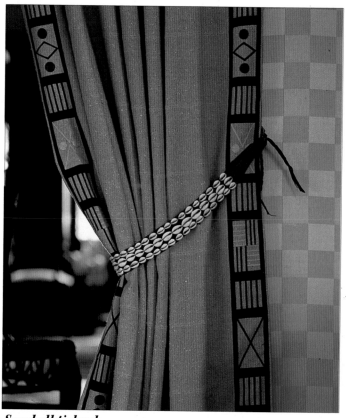

Seashell tieback
Rows of tiny white cowrie shells make an unusual but attractive tieback. They coordinate well with the pattern of the border fabric and add texture to the curtain. The shiny surface of the shells catches the light.

——— TRADITIONAL TIEBACKS ———

Single tassel jute tieback attached to wall

Double tassel jute tieback attached to wall

Silk and cotton tieback attached to wall

Jute plait attached to wall

POSITIONING TIEBACKS

The position of the tieback affects the way a curtain hangs.
The three main ways of placing tiebacks are shown below, but you
can experiment by trying it in different positions until the
curtain makes a shape that you like.

Around the pole
Looping a tieback around the curtain and over the pole gathers the fabric and brings the curtain's leading edge off the ground. This arrangement is best used where the curtain is not often moved.

Centre of the curtain
A tieback around the centre may be positioned part of the way down the curtain's length. The supporting hook is behind the curtain. Pull the curtain out above the tieback to give it shape.

Low down the curtain
Tiebacks positioned low on the curtain and fixed to the side of it should generally be set two thirds of the way down. If, however, you are using long tassels, lift the tieback higher.

ALTERNATIVE TIEBACKS

Rope twisted around
drape and tied

Tapestry band
around drape

Brass hook
attached to wall

Brass rosette
attached to wall

FABRIC GLOSSARY

THE NATURAL RAW MATERIALS that make up furnishing fabrics are cotton, linen, wool and silk. Each has its own characteristics and there are many variations within each type. In addition to these, there are manmade fibres, some of which are combined with natural materials to produce a blend. All fabrics, with the exception of one or two such as felt, are woven. They are produced on looms and, in the main, consist of weft threads (those that travel from side to side) and warp threads (those that travel up and down).

While some types of fabric are best for certain situations – flimsy muslin for privacy and light diffusion, tapestry for insulation – there are no hard and fast rules for choosing fabric for your windows. A selection is shown here, ranging from linings and basic fabrics, through neutrals, to coloured fabrics. Browse and be inspired.

Linings and basic fabrics

Interlining (thick)
This is made of combed cotton and comes in a variety of thicknesses. It is placed between fabric and lining in curtains to provide insulation as well as body and weight.

Lining
Standard lining is made of a tightly woven cotton fabric called sateen. This keeps its shape well, even after dry cleaning. Lining is generally used in cream or white, but it is also available in a range of colours.

Thermal lining
This is standard cotton lining that is coated with a layer of aluminium on one side for insulation. The coated side is silver-grey and should lie against the fabric. The other side is usually light-coloured.

Blackout lining
This is made up of one layer of opaque material between two layers. It blocks out all light and is best used with solid, opaque fabrics rather than those whose appeal depends on their translucency.

Calico
An inexpensive fabric, calico is raw unbleached cotton with a plain weave. It was originally used as a lining and backing fabric, but it is now popular for all kinds of window dressings.

Black and white ticking
A strong, tightly woven cotton, this is based on the fabric traditionally used to cover mattresses. This version is softer and less dense than mattress ticking, so is more easily draped.

Neutral and simple-patterned fabrics

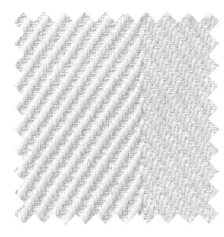

Herringbone cotton

A diagonally patterned, or herringbone, weave gives this heavy cotton its chunky texture. Strong and hard-wearing, it is a good choice for thick curtains.

French ticking

This closely woven cotton fabric is based on the traditional striped material used to cover mattresses. It is suitable for all kinds of window furnishings.

Cotton with open grid

Lightweight and almost sheer, this cotton fabric has a pattern of open gridwork embroidery across its surface. It works well for full curtains that do not need to exclude light.

Printed muslin

Muslin is a very fine, translucent cotton that is often plain. This version has a white printed design to add texture. Muslin can be hung behind curtains in daytime to provide privacy.

Cotton check

This is a simple but sturdy cotton fabric, suitable for all kinds of window furnishings. It may be lined and interlined, but, since it is the same front and back, it can also be used for unlined items.

Hessian

This open-weave, rough-textured fabric is made of fibre from the jute plant. It is generally plain, but this example has a coloured stripe woven into it. Hessian may be lined, but also works well on its own.

Chenille damask

Chenille is made from fluffy cotton yarn – the name comes from the French for hairy caterpillar – that gives it its soft texture. Here it is woven in damask style, with a raised pattern and flat background.

Natural linen

This beautiful fabric is made from flax. It is strong, hard-wearing and drapes well. Linen may be finely woven or, as here, have a more open weave. It can be dyed but looks its best in natural shades.

Coloured and patterned fabrics

Cotton and linen mix

The combination of cotton with stronger linen fibre makes a hard-wearing, slightly stiff fabric that is particularly suitable for flat blinds and edgings. The slightly raised motif adds texture.

Tapestry

Although machine-woven, this fabric possesses the ornate look of hand-woven tapestries, in which each stitch is individually made. With its rich texture and pattern, it is ideal for heavy curtains or blinds.

Heavy cotton weave

This thick, robust fabric is adorned with a fleur-de-lys pattern. It looks good from the front and back so would be suitable for unlined curtains and blinds.

Soft blanket

The combed wool used to make this blanket fabric makes it soft and warm. It provides good insulation at draughty windows. The same front and back, it does not need lining.

Wool damask

Like all damasks, this woollen fabric is woven to produce a raised pattern and flat background. Heavy, yet soft, it drapes well and provides good insulation. It can be used without lining.

Wool tartan

This woollen cloth is woven in plaids of different scale and patterns, each specific to a Scottish clan. Originally a clothing fabric, it is now often used for furnishings. It is warm, drapes well and may be used without lining.

Wool check

The twill or diagonal weave of this woollen cloth is produced by passing the weft threads alternately over one, then two warp threads. This smart-looking cloth is suitable for all kinds of window furnishings.

Paisley

The Paisley pattern is printed in many colours on a fine Egyptian cotton. Paisley originated in the East but was imported into the Scottish town of Paisley. It features swirling cone or pear shapes.

Cotton chintz
Chintz is a cotton fabric that generally features a multicoloured floral print on a cream or light ground. Beautiful designs such as this are often based on archive patterns.

Printed linen
Frequently used in its natural colour, linen can also have patterns printed on it. This example has a dynamic foliage pattern, screen-printed in at least eight colours. It is suitable for all kinds of window dressings.

Printed cotton
The background of this cotton has been overprinted to resemble a colour wash overlaid with gold. Although printed, the fabric looks similar to rich velvet from a distance, showing the versatility of cotton.

Silk taffeta
A brittle, finely woven fabric, taffeta has a crisp finish. The warp and weft threads of different colours give it an everchanging surface. It drapes well and is suitable for full-length curtains.

Silk damask
Silk is the traditional material for damask, which has a special weave that produces a raised pattern and flat background. Although fine, this beautiful and elegant fabric has body and so drapes well.

Checked silk
Silk is made from the soft, lustrous fibre made by silk worms for their cocoons. This checked silk has different coloured warp and weft threads, with further threads inlaid to create the grid effect.

Striped velvet
Velvet has a pile that generally absorbs, as well as reflects, light. The luxurious red stripe on this cotton example catches the light and shimmers against the matt gold of the background.

Printed velvet
Velvet always has a luxurious appearance. This example has a contemporary look and would work well as a smart, full-length lined curtain.

The Basic Techniques

MEASURING WINDOWS

FOR SUCCESSFUL WINDOW TREATMENTS, it is vital that you take careful measurements or all the hard work in making your curtain or blind will be wasted. Always use a steel tape measure – cloth measures do not give accurate enough measurements – and make clear, concise notes of measurements (it is worth making a habit of jotting down the width first so that you do not get measurements confused).

The first stage of measuring is to decide where the support should be if it is not already in place. There are three basic choices: you can hang curtains or blinds on a support attached to the wall above the frame and extending to each side; to a support attached to the window frame; or to a support within the window recess. If the support is attached to the wall or the window frame, then you must also decide whether you want your window treatment to stop at the level of the window sill or extend down to the floor.

Next you will need to determine the finished width and drop of your curtain or blind, and use these measurements to work out the actual, or cut, width and drop of fabric needed, by adding amounts for seams, headings and hems to the finished width and drop (see the tables on pp. 40–41). If using a patterned fabric, you must also allow extra fabric for matching the pattern across the fabric widths (see p. 41).

GLOSSARY OF MEASURING TERMS

Finished width: the width of the area the curtain or blind is to cover. The curtain or blind should make this width once it is pleated or gathered.

Finished drop: the length of the curtain or blind once it is completed and hung.

Cut width: the finished width plus allowances for seams and fullness for the heading.

Cut drop: the finished drop plus allowances for hems and headings.

Width of fabric: the width of the fabric as purchased. Generally, the width of fabric you are using will be less than the cut width of your curtain or blind and so you will need to buy more than one width and join them together.

Support: a device such as a pole, track or lath from which a curtain or blind hangs. It can be attached outside, on or within the frame.

Recessed window: a window that is set back into the wall, so that you can hang a curtain or blind inside the recess instead of on the wall.

Selvedge: the tightly woven edges of a width of fabric.

Measuring for a curtain or blind that hangs from a support on the wall

A support fitted to the wall is usually positioned 10–30 cm (4–12 in) above the window and extends up to 20 cm (8 in) to each side as space permits. Measure the width of the window and add the amount the support extends to each side to get the finished width (A). Measure the drop of the window and add the distance between the support and the top of the window to get the finished drop (B). If you are extending your curtains to the floor, also add the distance from the sill to the floor (B1) to get the finished drop.

Deduct 2.5 cm (1 in) from finished drop if curtain is to fall just short of floor. If curtain is to drape on floor, add up to 15 cm (6 in) depending on style.

Measuring for a curtain or blind that hangs from a support attached to the window frame

For a curtain or blind where the support is fitted to the frame, measure from one side of the frame to the other (C) to get the finished width, and from top of the frame to the sill (D) to get the finished drop. For floor-length curtains, measure from top of the frame to the floor (D plus D1) to get finished drop.

Measuring for a curtain or blind that hangs inside the window recess

For a curtain or blind where the support is fitted within the window recess, measure the distance from one side of the recess to the other (E) to get the finished width, and the distance from the top of the recess to the sill (F) to get the finished drop.

Deduct 2.5 cm (1 in) from finished drop if curtain is to fall just short of floor. If curtain is to drape on floor, add 15 cm (6 in).

Estimating fabric

Use the finished width and finished drop measurements you have made to work out the cut width and cut drop of your curtain or blind and then use them to estimate how much fabric you need to buy. Remember that if you are using a patterned fabric, you need to allow extra for matching the pattern across the widths (see p. 41).

1 To work out cut width for curtains, multiply finished width by amount of fullness your heading requires (see p. 40) and add amounts for side hems. For blinds, add amounts for seams, returns and other extras, such as pleats, (see p. 41) to finished width.

For example:
Finished width (132 cm/52 in): A, C or
  E on diagrams opposite and above
x *allowance for heading (2.5)*
= *330 cm/130 in*
+ *allowance for side hems (10 cm/4 in)*
= *cut width (340 cm/134 in)*

2 To work out cut drop for curtains, add amounts needed for top and base hems (see p. 40) to finished drop. For blinds, add amounts for base hem and for attaching top of blind to its support (see p. 41) to finished drop.

For example:
Finished drop (188 cm/74 in): B (+B1),
  D (+D1) or F on diagrams opposite
  and above
+ *allowance for top and base*
  hems (25 cm/10 in)
= *cut drop (213 cm/84 in)*

3 To calculate amount of fabric to buy, work out how many widths of fabric you need to make the required cut width. To do this, divide cut width by width of fabric you are using. Round up answer to nearest full number and multiply it by the cut drop to give the amount of metres (yards) of fabric to buy.

For example:
Cut width (340 cm/134 in)
÷ *width of fabric (122 cm/48 in)*
= *widths of fabric needed (2.8 = 3)*
Cut drop (213 cm/84 in) x 3
= *amount needed (639 cm/252 in).*
  For safety, buy 7 m/7½ yd.

Estimating for different curtain styles

This table tells you how much extra fabric you need to allow for different curtain styles. Once you have measured the finished width and the finished drop of your curtain (see pp. 38–39), you can work out the cut width and cut drop of your curtain by adding on the extra depending on the style of curtain you are making. Remember that most curtains require more than one width of fabric, so you also need to allow extra for joining fabric widths (see p. 43).

Heading type	Cut width See individual projects for details on side hems	Cut drop For each curtain	Notes
Slot heading	1½ to 2 times the finished width	The finished drop + 12 cm (4¾ in) for hem allowances + 3–5 cm (1½–2 in) for sleeve at top of curtain	This accommodates a slim pole of about 2 cm (¾ in) in diameter. Generally add about twice the circumference of the pole to the drop to allow for the slot.
Gathered heading 2.5-cm (1-in) tape	2½ times the finished width	The finished drop + 20 cm (8 in) for base hem + 5 cm (2 in) for top hem	There is only one row of pockets for the curtain hooks.
Pencil-pleat heading 7.5-cm (1-in) tape	2½ times the finished width	The finished drop + 20 cm (8 in) for base hem + 7.5 cm (3 in) for top hem	Hooks can be inserted into any one of three rows of pockets.
Hand-sewn hooks	1½ to 2 times the finished width	The finished drop + 20 cm (8 in) for base hem + 5 cm (2 in) for top hem	If a 'panel' effect is required, curtains headed with hand-sewn hooks need be little more than the width of the window.
Eyelets	1½ to 2 times the finished width	The finished drop + 20 cm (8 in) for base hem + 5 cm (2 in) for top hem	As a rule, eyelets should be set 10–15 cm (4–6 in) apart.
French or Goblet pleats	2½ times the finished width	The finished drop + 20 cm (8 in) for base hem + 18–20 cm (7–8 in) for top hem	This allows for about four or five pleats per fabric width.
Box pleats	3 times the finished width, if the whole width is to be box pleated 2–2½ times the finished width, if the pleats are to be spaced out	The finished drop + 20 cm (8 in) for base hem + 18–20 cm (7–8 in) for top hem	The width of the fabric must be divisible by the width of the front of one box pleat. For example, if a pleat measures 10 cm (4 in) across the front, the fabric has to be divided into equal 10-cm (4-in) spaces.

Estimating for different blind styles

This table is a guide to estimating fabric amounts for the main types of blind. Many flat blinds can be made within one standard fabric width, but wide or pleated blinds will need more. The measurements provided below are general guides. For specific instructions look at the instructions given for the blind projects.

Blind type	Cut width	Cut drop	Notes
Blind with lath top	Finished width + 10 cm (4 in) for side hems	Finished drop + 5 cm (2 in) for base hem + 25 cm (10 in) for attaching top of blind to the lath. If the blind has returns (see p. 56) allow 5 cm (2 in) for attaching fabric to lath.	Allow additional lining fabric for rod pockets. Each pocket measures 12 cm (4¾ in) long by the width of the blind.
Slot-head blind	Finished width + 10 cm (4 in) for side hems	Finished drop + 5 cm (2 in) for base hem + 7.5–25 cm (3–10 in) for sleeve at top, depending on size of pole.	Make sure you allow enough in the drop to make a comfortable sleeve for the pole.
Pleated blind	Finished width + 10 cm (4 in) for side hems + 10 cm (4 in) for returns + amount for each pleat, for example 20 cm (8 in)	Finished drop + 5 cm (2 in) for base hem + 25 cm (10 in) for attaching top of blind to the lath. If the blind has returns, see above.	Pleated blinds often look best with some fullness at the base so allow another 20 cm (8 in) on the drop.
Inverted pleat blind	Finished width + 20–30 cm (8–12 in) for central inverted pleat + 10 cm (4 in) for side hems + 4 cm (1½ in) for seams to join sides to central pleat	Finished drop + 5 cm (2 in) for base hem + 25 cm (10 in) for attaching the top of the blind to a lath. If the blind has returns, see above.	

Allowing for repeat patterns

The design on patterned fabric must line up exactly across joined widths. Take this into account when calculating fabric quantities – you need extra fabric because some is discarded in order to match the pattern.

Once you have calculated the cut drop (see pp. 38–39), measure the length of a complete pattern – this may be noted on the label with fabric. Divide the cut drop by the pattern length. Round up this number to the next full number and multiply by the pattern length to give the length that needs to be cut.

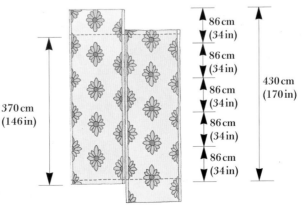

370 cm (146 in)

86 cm (34 in)
86 cm (34 in)
86 cm (34 in)
86 cm (34 in)
86 cm (34 in)

430 cm (170 in)

***For example**, if you have a cut drop of 370 cm (146 in) and a pattern length of 86 cm (34 in), divide 370 (146) by 86 (34) to get 4.3. Round this up to 5. Multiply the pattern length of 86 (34) by 5. This means that you will need to cut a length of 430 cm (170 in), so that you have enough to match up the pattern across widths.*

PREPARING FABRIC

Cutting fabric

Fabrics are usually supplied rolled around a cardboard tube, making them easier to handle when laying them out for cutting. Before cutting, check the fabric for any faults and double-check all measurements. Take great care when cutting – accuracy at this stage means fewer problems later on. Use sharp scissors, preferably with long blades, such as those used by professional curtain makers or dressmakers. A good quality pair will last for years.

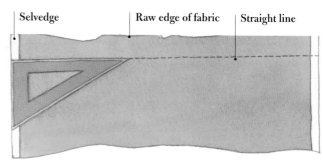

Selvedge | Raw edge of fabric | Straight line

1 *Straighten raw edge of fabric by using a T-square or any other right-angled object to make a straight line that is square to the selvedge.*

CUTTING SHEER FABRICS

When cutting sheer or loosely woven fabrics, draw out a thread across the width as a guide to help you cut straight. Cut along the path of this thread.

Thread drawn out across width of fabric

2 *To divide fabric into the cut drops required, first measure and mark the distance of the cut drop down the selvedge and down the centre of the fabric width. Make a line across the fabric by joining the marks with pencil or chalk, using a long rule. Repeat until you have marked all the cut drops needed and cut along the lines with sharp scissors.*

Straightened raw edge

Marks joined by line

Marks being joined by line

Mark showing drop

One cut drop

One cut drop

One cut drop

Combining widths and half widths

Once you have cut out your fabric, combine widths as necessary. If a pair of curtains requires three widths, cut one fabric width in half and make each curtain of one and a half widths (below left). If a blind needs more than one width, make the blind with one full width at the centre and a part width at each side (below).

Widths for curtains
If using part widths and full widths of fabric, always place the part width at the outside of the curtain and the full width at the centre.

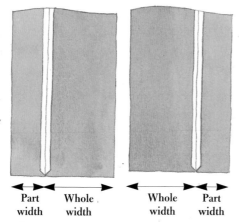

Part width | Whole width | Whole width | Part width

Widths for blinds
Avoid using narrow strips to make up the width of a blind. Cut down centre panel so that smaller sections are at least quarter fabric widths.

Part width | Whole width | Part width

Joining fabric widths

You can join together fabric widths for lined and interlined curtains or blinds by simply machine stitching the two widths together. For unlined curtains or blinds, use French seams (see p. 47) for joining widths so that the raw edges are neatly concealed.

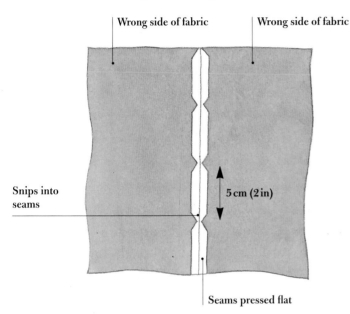

Wrong side of fabric   Wrong side of fabric

5 cm (2 in)

Snips into seams

Seams pressed flat

Place widths right sides together, leaving a seam allowance of 2.5 cm (1 in). Machine stitch parallel to the selvedge, or raw edge. Press seams flat. If fabric puckers when stitched or if selvedge appears tight, it may affect the way the fabric hangs. Snip into the seams at 5-cm (2-in) intervals to allow some give, but be careful to not cut into the stitching.

Weighting a curtain

Curtains, especially floor-length ones, hang best if they are weighted down with curtain weights that are stitched into the base hem. The weights help the curtain keep its shape, especially when it has a full heading.

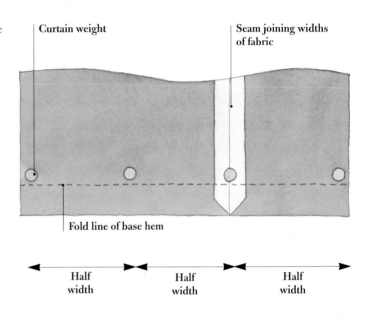

Curtain weight   Seam joining widths of fabric

Fold line of base hem

Half width   Half width   Half width

Insert weights at each corner of the curtain and at half-width intervals across its base. You should cover the weights in lining fabric and then stitch them into the base hem by hand (see p. 46).

Interlining and lining

Allow for the same amount of interlining and lining as the main fabric when estimating how much to buy – even though you use slightly less. If possible, buy lining in the same width as the main fabric so that seams match. Interlining seams are concealed by the lining so its width matters less.

Interlining
Join interlining widths with a lapped seam (see p. 47). Before starting to make the curtain, attach interlining to the main fabric, using locking-in stitch (see p. 44). Lock in the interlining at seams joining widths of fabric and halfway between fabric widths.

Lining
Cut and join lining widths as for fabric. Press seams flat. If possible, match joins of the lining with those of the fabric. On large curtains or wide blinds lock in lining as interlining.

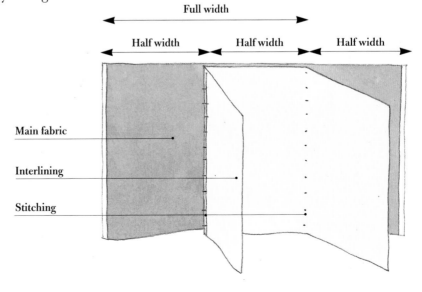

Full width

Half width   Half width   Half width

Main fabric

Interlining

Stitching

HAND STITCHES

Tacking stitch

This is a temporary stitch used to hold together several layers of fabric as a more secure alternative to pinning.

Thread secured with knot

1.25-cm (½-in) stitch

Secure thread with a knot and make a series of straight stitches, each about 1.25 cm (½ in) long. To remove the stitching, cut off the knot and pull out the thread.

Locking-in stitch

Use this stitch to secure lining or interlining loosely to the back of wide curtains or blinds and prevent the separate layers ballooning apart when they are hanging.

Interlining folded back

Thread secured with knot

Back of main fabric

15 cm (6 in)

Secure thread at back of interlining. Put needle through fold of lining close to edge and take up a few threads of the main fabric. Put needle through the loop of thread leaving some slack thread and make the next stitch about 15 cm (6 in) farther down.

Herringbone stitch

This neat stitch keeps hems that are to be covered by lining flat and in place. For right-handed people, stitches are worked from left to right with the needle pointing left.

Thread secured inside hem

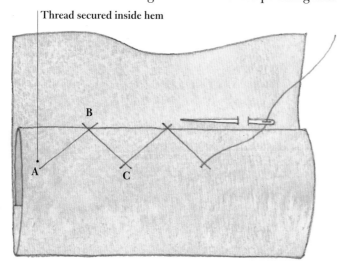

B

A

C

Working from left to right with the needle pointing left, secure thread inside hem and bring needle through hem edge (A). Make a small stitch in the fabric directly above hem edge and about 2.5 cm (1 in) to the right (B), with needle pointing left. Take the next stitch 2.5 cm (1 in) to the right in hem edge (C), again with needle pointing left. Repeat sequence of alternating stitches as shown until you reach end of hem.

Slipstitch

Use this stitch to sew a hem in place invisibly. Here, the size of the stitch is exaggerated so you can see how it works; in reality you should hardly be able to see it.

Thread secured inside hem

A

C B

Working from right to left, secure thread inside hem and bring needle out near folded edge. Insert needle into main fabric and make a small stitch (A). Catch only a few threads at a time so the stitching does not show on the right side. Insert needle back into fold about 3 mm (⅛ in) from first stitch (B). Pass needle through fold and bring out again about 1.25 cm (½ in) from first pair of stitches (C). Repeat the sequence.

Daisy chain stitch

This stitch consists of a small chain of threads that you can use to provide a loose link between lining and fabric at the base hem of a curtain and so prevent them from billowing apart.

Thread secured
inside hem

1 *Secure thread in hem with a couple of small stitches. Take a third stitch but do not pull it through. Leave the loop loose. Hold the loop around the first finger and thumb of your left hand (or right, if you are left-handed). Hold the needle, with thread attached, in your other hand.*

2 *Use the second finger of your left hand to pull the lower part of the thread held by your right hand through the loop.*

3 *Release your finger and thumb so that the loop tightens around thread as you pull on the thread with your right hand. Repeat to form a continuous chain of about 5 cm (2 in). When chain is right length, take needle through loop and pull tight to secure chain. Stitch end of chain to underside of lining hem.*

Stabbing stitch

Use this stitch to hold several layers of fabric together – for example at the base of a goblet pleat (see p. 51).

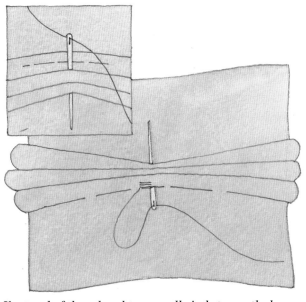

Knot end of thread and pass needle in between the layers so that the knot lies at the centre of the pleat (see inset). Pass the needle back and forth close to the same spot through all the layers, until you have a neat, firm stitch holding all the layers in place.

Couching stitch

Use this stitch to attach rings or hooks to fabric. Use a double thread for extra strength.

Using double thread, secure the thread in the fabric and make a simple stitch over and over in the same place until the ring is firmly attached. To attach a hook, make several groups of stitches all around the hook and pass the needle from one group of stitches to the next without breaking the thread (see inset).

HEMS AND SEAMS

Double curtain hem with interlining

Use this hem when adding interlining to a curtain. The double hem locks the interlining securely and neatly to the curtain before stitching the lining on top. Add in curtain weights at this stage if they are needed.

5-cm (2-in) side fold

10-cm (4-in) higher base fold

10-cm (4-in) lower base fold

Base

1 *Lay fabric right side down. At the base, fold up 10 cm (4 in) and press. Fold up by 10 cm (4 in) again and press. Press in 5 cm (2 in) at the sides. Open out the folds as above.*

Interlining folded up 10 cm (4 in)

Raw edges aligned

2 *Lay interlining on fabric, aligning edges of interlining with raw edge at sides and lower fold line along base of fabric. Fold interlining up 10 cm (4 in) and secure interlining to fabric along fold with herringbone stitch (see p. 44).*

Interlining folded in 5 cm (2 in)

Raw edge of interlining

3 *Fold interlining down again and press it in 5 cm (2 in) at the side. Herringbone stitch raw edge in place along lower fold line and along folded edge at fold line running up the side of the fabric.*

Base of fabric turned up and raw edge herringboned stitched in place

4 *At base of curtain, turn fabric up at first fold line and press. Herringbone stitch raw edge of fabric in place.*

Base corner folded in diagonally

Curtain weight

5 *Fold base corner in diagonally, aligning fold line at side of fabric with raw edge of base. Stitch in curtain weight if needed (see inset).*

Side hem folded in and herringbone stitched

6 *Fold in side hem of curtain again, along 5-cm (2-in) fold line. Press and herringbone stitch it in place.*

Base hem folded up and slipstitched

7 *Turn in second fold of base hem and press. Stitch across the mitred corner and secure base hem with slipstitch (see p. 44). Repeat Steps 5–7 to mitre corner at other side of fabric in the same way.*

Double lining hem

A double hem gives a firmer base to a lining and is useful in case the lining shrinks and needs to be let down.

Fold up 5 cm (2 in) at base of lining and press flat. Fold up base again to make a double 5-cm (2-in) hem. Press and machine along top, close to fold.

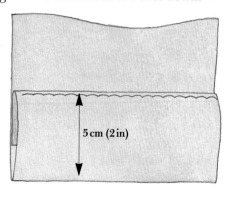

5 cm (2 in)

Covering curtain weights

Curtains hang best if they have weights along their base in the corners and at half-width intervals (see p. 43).

To cover a weight, place it on a piece of lining (near right). Fold lining over the weight and stitch around all sides (far right). Trim surplus and handstitch them into the corner hems (see Step 5 above).

Making a French seam

This seam is used for joining widths for an unlined curtain or blind. It hides the raw edges of the fabric.

Place pieces to be joined wrong sides together, matching any pattern, and tack together (see p. 44). Machine stitch 6 mm (¼ in) from raw edges (above left). Turn the fabric so that right sides are facing. Press and stitch 1 cm (⅜ in) away from folded edge, so that the raw edges are concealed inside the seam, making a neat finish (above right). Open the fabric out and press the seam flat on the wrong side. Remove tacking stitches.

Making a lapped seam

Use this seam to join together two widths of interlining.

Place both pieces of fabric to be joined right side up so that one overlaps the other by about 2 cm (¾ in). Machine stitch the two pieces together, using either a zigzag or a straight stitch.

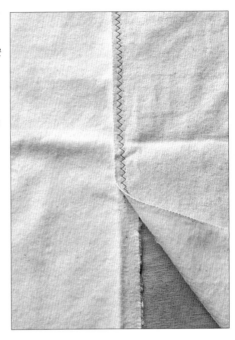

Making piping

Use piping to make a neat, practical finish along the side, top and bottom edges of both curtains and blinds. Cut your fabric on the bias so that it has the flexibility to stretch around curves and corners.

1 *To cut bias strips, first fold the fabric on the diagonal to mark the cross-grain (bias) of the fabric. Press the fold.*

2 *Open fold and, with fold line as guide, use pins to mark parallel lines 5 cm (2 in) apart, diagonally across fabric. Cut along lines to create 5-cm (2-in) wide strips.*

3 *Pin two strips right sides together as shown. The strips should be at right angles so that the straight grain matches at the short edges.*

4 *Machine stitch strips together beside the pins and press seam open. Trim off excess corners of fabric (see inset). Continue joining strips in this way to make the required length.*

5 *Fold strip in half lengthwise, wrong sides together. Place regular piping cord into the folded fabric. Using a piping or half foot, machine stitch edges of strip, keeping close to the cord.*

HEADINGS

Making a slot heading

For this heading, you make a 'sleeve' of fabric into which a slim pole goes. The slot can be at the top or set down (see Step 2).

1 *Fold over and press a double allowance at the top of curtain or blind. Allow for slot to be at least 1.25 cm (½ in) bigger than the circumference of pole. Machine stitch across the base.*

2 *For a slot lower down, fold over a double allowance 2.5 cm (1 in) deeper than in Step 1 and machine stitch 2.5 cm (1 in) from the top and across the base.*

Making a pencil pleat heading

This heading is made with 7.5-cm (3-in) tape, which gathers the curtain into pleats.

1 *Turn over a single hem at the top of the curtain. The hem should be less than 7.5 cm (3 in) so the raw edge is covered by tape. Align the tape with the top of curtain, tucking it under at each end but leaving the strings free. Knot strings at one end and secure them beneath the tape with several lines of machine stitching. Leave the strings at the other end free. Machine stitch along the top and bottom edges of the tape to attach it to the curtain.*

2 *Pull up loose strings of tape until the curtain is the required width. Make sure that pleats are evenly distributed across the width. Knot strings, but do not finally secure until you have checked the width of the curtain.*

3 *Place hooks in pockets, one at each end of the curtain and the rest about 7.5 cm (3 in) apart. The hooks are generally placed in the middle row of pockets on the tape. Alternatively, they can be placed in the top (see inset) or in the lower row.*

Making a gathered heading

This simple heading is made with 2.5-cm (1-in) tape, which is stitched to the back of the curtain.

Position the tape at least 2.5 cm (1 in) down from the top of curtain, the exact distance depending on the situation. Here, the top edge of the tape is set 5 cm (2 in) down. Follow the instructions for the pencil pleat heading (see Steps 1–3, p. 48) to attach the heading and prepare the curtain for hanging. With 2.5-cm (1-in) tape there is no choice in where you place the hooks since there is only one row of pockets.

Hand-sewing hooks

No tape is used on this heading. Instead, long hooks, usually brass, are hand-sewn directly to the back of the curtain.

Position hooks at the top of curtain, leaving about 15–20 cm (6–8 in) between each hook. The top of the hook should not project above top of curtain, unless hooks are intended to be seen (see left).

15–20 cm (6–8 in)

Making an eyelet heading

This heading is made with a punch and dye set. It punches a hole in the fabric and fits the two parts of the brass eyelet, one on each side of the fabric. Position them 1.25 cm (½ in) from curtain top at intervals of 7.5–13 cm (3–5 in).

1 *With the fabric right side down, place the punch underneath it at the position you want the eyelet. With its rounded side down, position the dye on top of it on the other side of the fabric and tap firmly with a hammer to make the hole.*

2 *Place the centre part of the eyelet under the fabric so that it projects through the hole from the right side (see inset). Place the ring over it and position the dye into it, pointed side down. Tap firmly with the hammer to fit into place and complete the eyelet.*

Making French pleats

This smart-looking heading is made up of groups of three pleats and is particularly suitable for floor-length curtains.

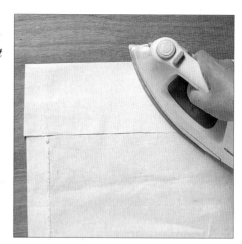

1 *Fold the top of the curtain over to the wrong side at the finished drop line and press. Here about 18 cm (7 in) of fabric is folded over.*

2 *Open out the fold. Take some fusible buckram about 10 cm (4 in) wide and 15 cm (6 in) longer than the width of the curtain. Place the fusible buckram across the top of the curtain so that its bottom edge aligns with the finished drop line.*

3 *Fold in the excess fusible buckram at each end. Fold the excess fabric at the top over the fusible buckram and press. The heat of the iron seals the fusible buckram to the fabric.*

4 *Fold over the covered fusible buckram so that the finished drop line is at the top of the curtain and press again.*

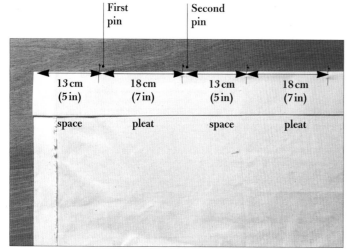

First pin Second pin

13 cm (5 in) 18 cm (7 in) 13 cm (5 in) 18 cm (7 in)

space pleat space pleat

5 *Mark positions of pleats with pins. The distance between the edge of the curtain and the start of the first pleat is generally the same as the space between each pleat. This should be about 10–15 cm (4–6 in) but can be adjusted to suit your curtain. Here, the space between each pleat is 13 cm (5 in) and amount allowed for each pleat is 18 cm (7 in).*

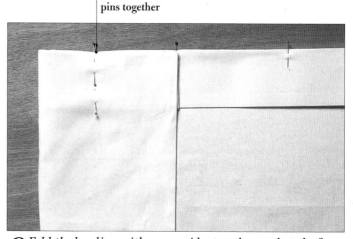

First and second pins together

6 *Fold the heading with wrong sides together so that the first pin meets the second pin. Pin in place. Take the third pin to the fourth pin and continue to fold and pin the remaining pleats in the same way. Machine stitch each pleat from the top of the curtain to the base of fusible buckram section.*

7 *Turn curtain over so right side is uppermost. Flatten pleat and pinch the middle into a pleat (see inset). Bring up material at each side to make three pleats of equal size.*

8 *Secure base of pleat with stabbing stitch (see p. 45). At top of pleat, stitch each of the three folds in place. Repeat Steps 7–8 to make the remaining pleats.*

Making goblet pleats

This elegant heading consists of pleats that are spaced out along the top of the curtain. They are stuffed to keep their shape.

1 *Follow Steps 1–6 for French pleats (see p. 50) and, with fabric right side up, pinch base of pleat together and secure with stabbing stitch (see p. 45).*

2 *Leave top of pleat open and stuff it with a roll of wadding. Push wadding well down into the pleat to give it shape. Repeat with rest of pleats.*

Making box pleats

These hand-sewn pleats give an attractive neat finish, but are not suitable for heavy fabrics.

First pin   Second pin

10 cm (4 in)   10 cm (4 in)

1 *Divide width of curtain into equal spaces, marked with pins on the front. The example here shows pins 10 cm (4 in) apart, to make box pleats measuring 10 cm (4 in) across the front.*

First and second pins together

2 *With the front of the curtain facing you, take the first pin to meet the second pin.*

Third pin

3 *Then take the third pin to meet the second pin and pin them in place to make a pleat.*

Fourth and fifth pins

4 *Take fourth pin to meet fifth pin and sixth pin to meet fifth pin to make a second pleat. Repeat the process until you have pinned all the pleats.*

5 *Press pleats across top of curtain and machine stitch across all the pleats, about 2.5 cm (1 in) down from the top of the curtain, to keep them in place.*

INSTALLATION TECHNIQUES
Putting up a pole

Poles are supported on wooden or metal brackets that are fitted to the wall above the window or to the window frame itself. If there is space, the pole should extend to each side so that the curtain can be pulled back off the window. Curtain rings are threaded onto the pole, with one at each end beyond the bracket to hold the curtains in place. For single curtains, place a ring outside the bracket at one end only, so the curtain can be pulled right back. Poles are available in many different styles and thicknesses and, if wooden, can be cut to the width required for your window. The instructions here give a general guide to putting up poles that you can adapt to your particular situation. Most poles also come with manufacturer's instructions that explain exactly how to fix the brackets and pole.

1 *Mark the position of the pole above the window. This distance should be about 10–15 cm (4–6 in), but will vary according to the situation.*

2 *Mark the position of the brackets to each side of the window, making sure they are aligned. These should be placed about 10 cm (4 in) from the architrave.*

3 *Fix one bracket to the wall following manufacturer's instructions. Wooden ones have a metal wallplate that is fixed to the wall first (see inset) and then the bracket is screwed onto the wallplate.*

4 *Check the pole in position on one bracket, ensuring it is straight. Fix other bracket. Tighten screws on underside of brackets into the pole to keep it firmly in place. Leave end rings off the pole.*

5 *Put one curtain ring on each end of pole beyond bracket. Fit finials to each end of pole so that ring is between the bracket and finial. Then you are ready to hang the curtains.*

Pole with architrave bracket
As well as being suitable for use on a wall, architrave brackets are thin enough to fit on the frame of a window. You need them when there is no room to fit brackets above or to the sides of a window or when the wall is too crumbly to support the weight of curtains. They are usually made of brass or other metal and you fit them to the frame with matching screws. Simply position the bracket, mark the screw holes, drill the holes and attach the bracket with screws. The front of the bracket screws into the pole to keep it in place.

Putting up a pole in a window recess

There are special brackets, known as 'thimble' brackets, for fitting a slim pole in a window recess. These encase each end of the pole and are completely hidden by, for example, a slot-head curtain. There are also brackets for attaching the ends of poles to a side wall when there is no room to attach it to the wall the window is in (see Step 3).

1 *Mark the position of the brackets on the sides of the recess – the distance down depends on the amount of fabric above the slot. Fit the brackets with the screws provided.*

2 *Measure the distance between the two brackets and cut the pole to about 3 mm (⅛ in) less than this distance. Fit the pole into the brackets and screw in the sleeve part of the bracket to hold the pole in place.*

3 *The result is an extremely neat fitting that can be used for a light-weight curtain with small rings or a slot heading. For a larger pole, fixed to an adjacent wall at one end, use a recess holder bracket (see inset).*

USING A TRACK

There are many types of tracks available that can be fitted either to the wall above the window or along the top of the window frame. The simplest type (see below) has small wall brackets that are screwed into the wall at regular intervals and then the track, which has gliders for hooks, simply clips into the bracket. If you put up track yourself, make sure you follow the manufacturer's instructions carefully. If you need to bend track around a curved or bay window, or conceal it behind a fascia, it is advisable to get it fitted by a professional.

Bracket screwed into wall

Track clipped into brackets

Gliders for attaching hooks

Cording a blind

The basic principles of cording a blind are the same whatever the type. Two or three lengths of cord are knotted to rings attached at or near the base of the blind and run up the back of the blind through a series of rings and eventually a screw eye attached to the lath at the top of the blind. The cords then all go across the top to one side of the blind, where the loose ends are threaded through a brass drop weight. To raise the blind, you pull the drop weight downwards and wind the excess cord around a cleat attached to the wall to keep the blind in a raised position.

Roman blind (see pp. 96–99)

This blind has dowel rods that run across the back of the blind at regular intervals. They sit in pockets (see p. 98) that are stitched to the lining.

1 Position the lowest rod pocket 10 cm (4 in) above the base of the blind and space them at intervals of 20–30 cm (8–12 in), with the highest one at least 35 cm (14 in) from the top.

2 Handstitch rings to the pockets up the centre of blind and a row 5 cm (2 in) from both edges.

3 Attach the screw eyes to the lath (see p. 55), directly in line with the rows of rings. Attach another screw eye 2.5 cm (1 in) in from the edge of the lath on the side where the pull strings will be.

4 Use one piece of cord for each row of rings. Attach each cord to bottom ring and thread it through rings above, through screw eye at top and through adjacent screw eyes to reach the additional screw eye at the end of the lath.

5 With cords taut, pass them into drop weight. Trim off any excess and secure with a knot.

Lath at top of blind

Screw eyes – one for each row of rings, plus one

Rings set 5 cm (2 in) in from blind edge

Dowel rod in rod pocket

Cord running up through rings

Cords attached to brass drop weight

Cord knotted to lowest ring

Panel blind (see pp. 108–111)

This blind has no dowel rods and only two rows of rings.
• Position each row of rings 10 cm (4 in) from sides and space them at intervals of about 15 cm (6 in), with the lowest one 5 cm (2 in) from the base and highest one at least 20 cm (8 in) from the top.

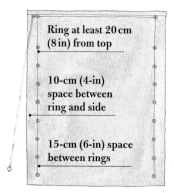

Ring at least 20 cm (8 in) from top

10-cm (4-in) space between ring and side

15-cm (6-in) space between rings

Panel blind with rod (see pp. 104–107)

This blind is like the panel blind (above) but has a dowel rod along the base.
• Position rod 15 cm (6 in) above base and position rings as with panel blind except that lowest ring in each row should be 15 cm (6 in) above rod.

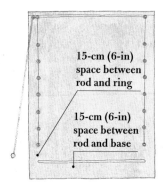

15-cm (6-in) space between rod and ring

15-cm (6-in) space between rod and base

Inverted pleat blind (see pp. 112–117)

This blind has two rows of rings and no dowel rods.
• Position each row of rings 10 cm (4 in) from sides and space them at about 30-cm (12-in) intervals, with the lowest one 5 cm (2 in) from the base and highest one at least 45 cm (18 in) from the top.

Ring at least 45 cm (18 in) from top

10-cm (4-in) space between ring and side

30-cm (12-in) space between rings

Blind with several inverted pleats (see pp. 118–123)

This blind has extra rows of rings running up each pleat.
• Position as for inverted pleat blind, adding extra rows of rings as required.

Fixing a lath to a blind

A lath for a blind is generally a 5- x 2.5-cm (2- x 1-in) piece of timber, cut to the finished width of the blind. Slimmer laths, measuring 2.5 x 2.5 cm (1 x 1 in), can be used for lightweight blinds. For covering a 5- x 2.5-cm (2- x 1-in) lath, allow at least 25 cm (10 in) of fabric above the finished drop line of the blind.

1 *Cut two pieces of the blind fabric about 7.5 cm (3 in) square. Wrap one piece around the end of the lath and, using a staple gun, fix it to the top and bottom of the wide face.*

2 *On the narrow faces of the lath, fold the fabric over neatly like a parcel and staple in place. Repeat at other end. If the blind is to be ceiling-fixed, drill screw holes through the lath (see p. 56).*

3 *Mark the finished drop line on the wrong side of the blind. Position the lath so that the bottom of it aligns with the marked drop line (top of blind).*

4 *Roll the lath away from the finished drop line towards the top of the blind. Roll it over once completely so that the same side as before is face up.*

5 *Fold the fabric extending above over the lath, trimming off any excess if necessary. Staple the fabric to the lath.*

6 *Roll the lath back towards the marked drop line until it rests in the correct position, with the top of the lath at the marked drop line.*

7 *Using a bradawl, mark the positions of screw eyes for cording the blind. These should align with the rows of cording rings on the blind.*

8 *Insert the screw eyes into the marked holes. Make sure that they are not too tight or they will pull on the fabric.*

Covering a lath for a blind with returns

Use this method when the rows of cording rings are close to the sides of the blind and you want to hide them with a return. The lath itself is neatly covered in lining fabric and the blind fabric extends around the ends of the lath. For this type of fixing you need to allow for an extra 5 cm (2 in) of fabric above the finished drop line.

1 *To cover a standard 5- x 2.5-cm (2- x 1-in) lath, cut a piece of lining material about 18 cm (7 in) wide by the length of the lath plus about 10 cm (4 in) for turning over the ends. Wrap this around the lath, turning under the raw edges and staple in place. Fold over the fabric at each end like a parcel and staple in place (see inset).*

2 *Position the blind, right side up, on the wide face of the covered lath, leaving about 5 cm (2 in) at each end to fold around the side of the lath. Staple the fabric to the lath.*

3 *Wrap the return at either end neatly around the end of the lath as shown and staple in place. Repeat at other end and insert screw eyes as in Steps 7–8 of 'Fixing a lath to a blind' (see p. 55).*

Ceiling-fixing a lath

You can fix a blind to the ceiling simply by inserting a screw through the lath into the ceiling above. This is particularly useful when you want to hang a blind at the front of a recess or when there is not enough room on the window frame to use angle brackets (see p. 57). Use wall plugs to make the fixing more solid.

1 *Before the lath is covered, mark the positions of screw holes at least 10 cm (4 in) from each end on the wide surface of the lath. Avoid the positions for screw eyes. Drill holes through the lath.*

2 *Having covered the lath (see p. 55) and cut away the fabric to reveal the drilled holes, place the lath in position and mark the screw holes in the ceiling. Drill holes in the ceiling and, using wallplugs, insert screws through the lath and into the ceiling as shown.*

3 *Here, the finished blind hangs flush with the front of the recess, giving a neat finish. You could also use this method to attach a blind directly to the ceiling in a room.*

Face-fixing a lath on angle brackets

The completed lath, with blind, is supported on angle brackets fixed to the sides of the window or wall.
The example shown here is in a recess, but the same method applies for face-fixing a lath to a wall.

1 *Take the completed blind and lath and position it above the window. Mark the base of the lath on each side as a guide for fixing the brackets.*

2 *Position the bracket so the top aligns with the pencil mark for the base of the lath. Mark the positions of the screw holes. Repeat at the other side of the window.*

3 *Drill the holes and position the bracket so that the top aligns with the pencil mark. Insert the screws and tighten. Repeat at the other side of the recess.*

4 *Place the blind into the recess so that the lath rests on the fixed brackets. Mark the position of the screw hole in the bracket on the base of the lath. Repeat at the other side.*

5 *Take the blind off the brackets. Insert a bradawl through the fabric and into the lath at the marked point. Repeat at the other end of the lath.*

6 *Put the lath back into place on top of the brackets and insert screws through the bracket and into the lath at each end to fix the blind in place.*

The Projects

UNLINED CURTAINS

THESE ARE the simplest curtains of all – panels of fabric that hang from a slim pole stretching across the top of the window. The curtains have double hems at the sides and base and a sleeve along the top through which the pole is slotted.

The curtains can be pushed open to the sides of the window, but a shimmery translucent fabric – such as the cream cotton muslin used here – admits enough light for them to stay permanently pulled closed if desired.

Type of window

• This style of curtain suits almost any type of window or space. It works particularly well on small windows where you should avoid elaborate treatments, or larger windows where you want to keep the look simple.

• Use sheer curtains as a decorative element on their own or to hang behind a set of heavy outer curtains. If making floor-length curtains, allow plenty of excess length so that they trail on the ground – this type of curtain looks unattractive suspended above the floor.

• Unlined sheer curtains make excellent light diffusers. Use them to protect furniture or other fabrics in the room from strong sunlight, or to obscure an unappealing view.

Type of fabric

• Choose plain fabrics or a fabric that looks the same front and back, such as cotton gingham. Avoid fabrics that show the workings of a complicated weave or printed pattern on the back.

• Heavy, open-weave, textured fabrics, such as hessian or scrum, also make excellent unlined curtains.

Options

• Vary the look of these curtains by using 2.5-cm (1-in) heading tape to create a gathered effect and by hanging the curtain on a pole with rings.

• Instead of using a sheer fabric that lets the light in, try traditional checked blankets for warmth and cosiness.

• Make slim borders down the leading edges to add colour and contrast.

WHAT YOU WILL NEED

Fabric for each curtain

Width

*Finished width of curtain (see pp. 38–39),
plus 8 cm (3 in) for hem allowances*

Length

*Finished drop of curtain (see pp. 38–39),
plus 12 cm (4¾ in) for hem allowances, plus
allowance for slot at the top (see p. 40)*

Accessories

Pole

*Slim pole cut to fit within the window space and
attached to the sides of the recess with thimble
brackets (see p. 53)*

Making the curtains

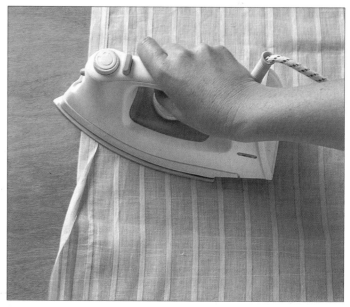

1 *When working with sheer or very light fabrics, provide a
visual guide to ensure that hems are straight and square by
marking a line on the fabric with a pencil and pulling out a
thread across the width.*

2 *Place the fabric right side down and fold over double
2-cm (¾-in) hems along each side and press. Pin the
side hems in place.*

3 *Fold over a double 5-cm (2-in) hem
at the base of the curtain, press and
pin the hem in place.*

4 *Machine stitch the hems at each side
of the curtain, making sure that the
hems are even and the stitching straight.*

5 *Machine stitch the base hem of the
curtain, again making sure that the
stitching is straight.*

Raw edge pressed
over by 2 cm (¾ in)

7-cm
(2¾ in)
slot
allowance

6 *At the top of the curtain, press over the raw edges 2 cm (¾ in). Then press over a further amount for your slot allowance (see p. 48) and pin in position. The allowance here is 7 cm (2¾ in).*

7 *Machine stitch along the top of the curtain 2 cm (¾ in) in from the edge and again along the base of the folded section to form the slot for the pole. Repeat Steps 2–7 to make the second curtain, slot the curtains on the pole and insert the pole into brackets (see p. 53).*

VARIATION ON UNLINED CURTAINS

Instead of a sheer fabric, a thick woollen blanket cloth was used for these curtains, providing a warm and cosy feel. Blanket cloth is good fabric to use for unlined curtains since it is the same front and back. In place of a slot heading, these curtains have hooks attached to the back along the top (see p. 49) and they hang from rings on a plain wooden pole.

CONTRAST-LINED CURTAIN

IN MEDIEVAL TIMES heavy textile hangings were often draped across cold walls or doorways to keep out draughts. Most homes have efficient heating systems these days and little or no need for draught excluders. But this style of panelled curtain, supported on hand-sewn hooks, lends a touch of historic grandeur and elegance to your home.

The example shown here (opposite) is made from a width of heavy embroidered chenille and hangs from a solid wooden pole mounted above the doorway. The tasseled tieback gives the curtain shape and keeps it off the doorway for access. Since the curtain is seen from both sides we have lined it with an equally attractive plainer but toning chenille.

Type of window

• This curtain is not used over windows but within the house. It has two 'fronts', both of which are on view.
• This type of double-sided curtain is also useful as a room divider. It does not have to extend across the entire room and can hang on a short pole projecting from a wall at right angles. You can use a heavy curtain hung in this way to break up a large area or create a backdrop for furniture.
• Part of a large landing or hallway can sometimes serve as a small room or additional work space. A double-sided curtain screens the space when needed, without the permanence of a door or a wall.

Type of fabric

• Heavy fabric is most effective for this type of curtain – and best for excluding draughts.
• Choose fabric and lining that work well together. But bear in mind that the rooms or spaces on each side of the curtain may be decorated in different colours or styles. The same pattern used in one colour on one side and in another on the other can look very effective.
• Make sure that the fabrics you choose are alike in weight since they are sewn edge to edge. If one is much heavier it will drag on the other.

Options

• Instead of the discreet heading shown in this example, try using chunky eyelets punched across the top of the curtain. Slot a pole through the eyelets. Alternatively, you can use tab or ribbon headings, but make sure they are strong enough to support the weight of the heavy curtain material.
• For added colour and texture, you could make borders or edgings on one or both sides of the curtain.
• Look at different styles of tieback, such as silk ropes and tassels, curly wrought iron or natural jute.

——— WHAT YOU WILL NEED ———

Main fabric for curtain

Width
Finished width of curtain (see pp. 38–39), plus 4 cm (1½ in) for hems

Length
Finished drop of curtain (see pp. 38–39), plus 4 cm (1½ in) for hems

Lining fabric for curtain

Width
As for main fabric

Length
As for main fabric

Accessories

Hooks
Finished width of curtain, divided by 20 if working in centimetres and 8 if working in inches, plus 1. Make sure the hooks are strong enough to support the fabric

Pole
At least 90 cm (36 in) wider than the doorway so that it extends at least 45 cm (18 in) on each side

Making the curtain

1 Place the main fabric and lining on a flat surface with right sides together. Match the raw edges at each side and pin them together, 2 cm (¾ in) in from the edge.

2 Machine stitch the main fabric and lining together at the sides, stopping 2 cm (¾ in) short of the top and base. Leave the top and base unstitched and turn the curtain right side out.

3 Having pressed the side edges, making sure that the curtain aligns along the top and the pattern is straight on both sides, press under 2-cm (¾-in) hems at the top of the main fabric and lining. Press under hems at the base of the curtain in the same way, again making sure the pattern is straight.

4 Secure the main fabric and lining together at the top of the curtain using slipstitch (see p. 44). Repeat at the base.

5 Position hooks across curtain top on lining side, with one in each corner and the rest at 20-cm (8-in) intervals. Place them near the top, but not showing from the front. Stitch them in place by hand with couching stitch (see p. 45).

6 *To attach the pole to the wall and hang the curtain, see instructions on p. 52. If you want to be able to pull the curtain back from the doorway, make sure that the final ring on one side is inside the wall bracket. If you want the curtain to remain always in the same position, covering the top of the doorway, keep the last ring outside the wall bracket as shown here (see right).*

VARIATIONS ON SIMPLE HEADINGS

Both of these curtains (see below) demonstrate how effective a simple approach can be. Like the contrast-lined curtain, they have headings without pleats or tape, even though they are made from much lighter fabrics. In place of hooks they are attached to their respective poles by ties knotted through the small rings, allowing them to hang loosely. To add definition and form, each curtain has a border in the same fabric as the ties.

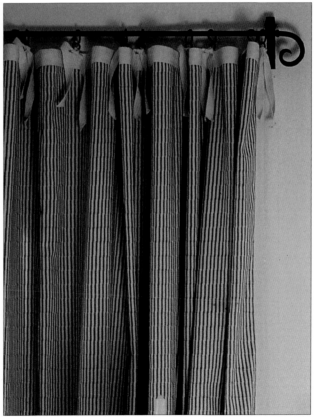

SINGLE CURTAIN WITH BOX PLEATS

ALLOW THE FABRIC TO SPEAK FOR ITSELF with this striking, unlined curtain. Despite a box-pleated heading, the curtain is essentially a panel that hangs from a simple wrought-iron pole. The heading, finished with a contrasting border in wool tartan, makes a flat, neat top but allows some fullness lower down the pleats, especially when the curtain is more than floor length. The curtain is attached to the pole by hooks hand-sewn to the border, and the pole extends sufficiently to the side of the door so that the curtain can be pulled out of the way if necessary.

Type of window

• In some situations, a single curtain is more effective than a pair, such as on windows that abut walls or on single doors. A single curtain at each of a pair of windows helps to maximise light and is simpler than hanging two pairs.

• On a staircase where a tall window is set asymmetrically in the wall space, a single curtain covering part of the adjoining wall as well as the window helps to create a better visual balance in the area.

• Put box-pleated headings on view, not behind pelmets, but remember that they work best when flat across most of the top since they look less attractive when bunched up.

Type of fabric

• Choose a fabric that suits the tailored, disciplined look of this box-pleated curtain. Plain fabrics and simple stripes both work well.

• Avoid using a fabric with complex patterns that would look messy once pleated.

• Crisp fabrics, such as cotton and linen, pleat well and stay in pressed folds. Bulky or very soft fabrics do not, so are less suitable for this curtain.

• If the curtain is to be unlined, like the one shown here, use a fabric that looks good from both sides.

Options

• The box pleats shown here are folded edge to edge and are held in place by the border across the top. To create a different look, open out the heading by putting a space between each pleat.

• For a more dramatic curtain, you can make the spaces (or the pleats) in a contrasting fabric. Join strips of fabric together carefully before making the curtain and pressing the pleats in place.

• For a quick way of pleating, press the heading into pleats but do not stitch. Then, simply use clips to hold the pleats in place and fix the curtain to the pole.

WHAT YOU WILL NEED

Main Fabric for curtain

Width

Finished width of curtain (see pp. 38–39), plus allowance for box pleats (see p. 40), plus 8 cm (3 in) for double side hems

Length

Finished drop of curtain (see pp. 38–39), plus 10 cm (4 in) for base hem, plus 2 cm (¾ in) for seam at the top

Fabric for contrasting border

Width

Finished width of curtain (see pp. 38–39), plus 5 cm (2 in) for seams

Length

Twice the finished border depth, plus 4 cm (1½ in) for seams. The border shown here is 5 cm (2 in) wide

Accessories

Hooks

Finished width of the curtain, divided by 15 if working in centimetres and 6 if working in inches, plus 1

Pole

At least 90 cm (36 in) wider than the doorway so that it extends at least 45 cm (18 in) on each side

Curtain weights

1 for each corner, plus 1 for each width of fabric (see p. 43)

Making the curtain

1 *When making wide unlined pleated curtains you will need to join fabric widths with French seams (see also p. 47). First place the two pieces of fabric wrong sides together, pin a 2-cm (¾-in) seam and machine stitch in place.*

2 *Turn the fabric to the right side and press. Pin the right sides together so that the raw edges of the seam are concealed and the seam has a neat finish. Machine stitch.*

3 *With right side down, turn and press over a double 2-cm (¾-in) hem down both sides of the curtain.*

4 *Turn and press a double 5-cm (2-in) hem along the base of the curtain (see p. 46).*

5 *Hand-sew a covered weight into each corner (see p. 46) and at the base of each of the seams joining fabric widths.*

6 *Pin both the side hems in place and secure them with machine stitching.*

7 *Machine stitch the base hem, taking care not to run the needle over the covered weights inside the hem.*

Making the box pleats

1 To mark positions of box pleats, measure in from one edge the width of one pleat front (see p. 51) and mark with a pin. Here, each pleat front is 10 cm (4 in) wide.

2 Measure from there the space allowed for fabric to be folded behind (double the width of pleat front) and mark with a pin. Here, the space is 20 cm (8 in).

3 Measure and mark width for next pleat front and then space allowed for fabric folded behind. Continue to repeat the process until you reach the other edge of the curtain. You will finish with a width for a pleat front.

4 To provide guides for folding the pleats, measure and mark with a pin the centre spot between the first and second pin.

5 Measure and mark the centre spot between the third and fourth pins in the same way and continue until you have measured and marked all of the widths of fabric to be folded behind.

6 Starting from one side, fold the fabric so that you bring the first pin to meet what is now the second pin (the pin that you inserted between the first and second pin in Step 4). Then bring what is now the third pin back to meet the second pin as well. Press the folds in place. Repeat to fold and press other pleats across the width of the curtain, folding the fabric so that what is now the fourth pin meets the fifth pin, the sixth meets the fifth and so on.

Total width of curtain before pleating

10 cm (4 in) 10 cm (4 in) 10 cm (4 in) 10 cm (4 in) 10 cm (4 in) 10 cm (4 in) 10 cm (4 in) 10 cm (4 in)

20 cm (8 in) 20 cm (8 in) 20 cm (8 in) 20 cm (8 in) 20 cm (8 in) 20 cm (8 in) 20 cm (8 in)

Curtain edge

First pin
Second pin
Third pin Fourth pin

Front of pleat
Fabric folded behind

Attaching the border

1 *With right sides together, place the contrasting border along the top of the curtain 2.5 cm (1 in) from the edge. Pin and machine stitch along it 5 cm (2 in) from the top edge – 2.5 cm (1 in) down from the edge of the border. This attaches the border to the curtain and holds the pleats in place.*

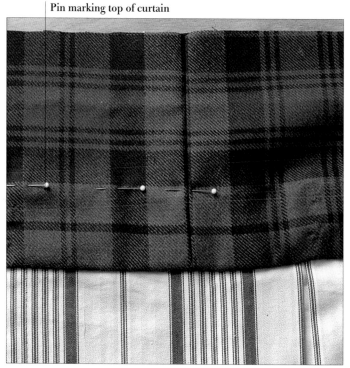

Pin marking top of curtain

2 *Fold the border back over itself so that it covers the top of the curtain. Mark with pins the line of the top of the curtain (which is hidden underneath the border).*

3 *Place the curtain right side down. Press the border over to the wrong side along the pinned fold line, pressing under the raw edge 2.5 cm (1 in) to form the hem.*

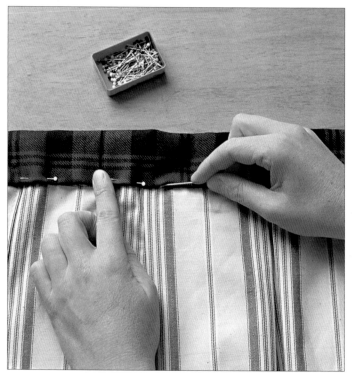

4 *Pin the border in place, turning under the raw edges at each end and slipstitch (see p. 44) it to the back of the curtain.*

Attaching the hooks

Hook 2 cm (¾ in) from edge   15 cm (6 in)   Pin marking position for next hook

1 *Position the first curtain hook 2 cm (¾ in) in from one end of the curtain. Place another hook 2 cm (¾ in) from the other end and use pins to mark the spaces for the remaining hooks in between. Allow about 15 cm (6 in) between each hook.*

2 *Use a couching stitch (see p. 45) to attach each of the hooks to the curtain securely, stitching through all layers of fabric in the border and the curtain. Put up the pole and hang the curtain (see p. 52).*

VARIATION ON CURTAIN WITH BOX PLEATS

The box pleats on these floor-length curtains are spaced out (see p. 40) to give a very different look. Instead of having a border and hooks at the top, they are attached to the pole with clips that also keep the pleats in position.

TARTAN LOOSE DRAPE

IF YOU HAVE AN INTERESTING window or French windows that you would like to make into a focal point, you can drape it with a length of unlined fabric, which allows light in and frames the view. The draped fabric is held by sewn rings, which fit over the stems of the rosettes fixed at the outermost points, and by a looped braid and tassel in the centre. The fabric falls into shape under its own weight.

Type of window

• Tall, rather than wide, windows are best for this kind of fabric draping. The proportions of the window and drape need to be in harmony for this arrangement to work.
• Do not overload small windows – allow the 'tails' of the fabric to fall only part way down each side, not to the floor.
• The drape does not close, so the window will be permanently on view. Bear this in mind both in terms of decor and of privacy and security.

Type of fabric

• Choose fabrics that are the same on both sides, such as this richly patterned wool tartan. Reversible fabrics are also suitable.

• Choose a fabric that drapes well and does not fall into stiff folds. The arrangement should be fluid with the fabric doing all the work.

Options

• To give the drape a different look, use flat braids or ribbons in contrasting or harmonious colours to swag up the centre of the drape. Loop them over a small hook and tie them in a knot or sew the ends together around the fabric.

WHAT YOU WILL NEED

Fabric for drape

Width
About 70 cm (27½ in), plus 8 cm (3 in) for hems

Length
Twice finished drop (see pp. 38–39), plus distance between rosettes (usually width of window frame), plus 50 cm (20 in) to allow fabric to drape on floor, plus 8 cm (3 in) for hems

Accessories

Brass rings
3 brass rings up to 1.25 cm (½ in) diameter

Brass hook
1 for central ring

Rosettes
2

Making the drape

Press under and stitch double 2-cm (¾-in) hems all around the fabric. Mark the position of the rings on the fabric. Place one in the centre and one at each side to match the position of the drape rosettes. Position the drape over the rosettes as shown opposite.

Finished drop of curtain – here, 273 cm (107½ in) – plus 25 cm (10 in) for draping on floor

Distance between rosettes – here, 241 cm (95 in)

Finished drop of curtain – here, 273 cm (107½ in) – plus 25 cm (10 in) for draping on floor

Brass ring   Brass ring   Brass ring

70 cm (27½ in)

Double 2-cm (¾-in) hem around all edges   Centre of fabric

VARIATIONS ON TARTAN LOOSE DRAPE

Antique rosettes
Choose different styles and finishes of rosette to suit the fabric and other furnishings. Here, an antique rosette in wood perfectly complements the tartan fabric.

Contrast braid
A length of braid is looped around the centre of the drape, pulling it into shape. The silky lustre of the braid contrasts with the matt finish of the woollen tartan.

GATHERED CURTAINS

BAY WINDOWS can be difficult to curtain, mainly because their angles preclude the use of some types of headings. Poles can be used, but they usually have to be fitted in three sections and the brackets then interfere with the pulling of the curtains. Here, a metal track bent to fit the bay is used to hold the curtains. A discreet cord and pulley mechanism allows the curtains to be pulled around the window. The track is a practical, not decorative, device and it is concealed by a lath and fascia covered in the same fabric as the curtains so that they blend in. The curtains are lined with a contrasting fabric and gathered onto a 2.5-cm (1-in) tape. Interlining adds extra warmth and fullness.

Type of window

• These curtains suit tall wide windows, which allow scope both for fabrics with large patterns and for more random designs, such as toile de Jouy, that work best over a wide expanse.

• They are useful where there is little room above the window for a pole, such as in a bay or where the window is close to the ceiling. Bear in mind that metal curtain tracks need to be put up professionally since special tools are required for bending the track around corners.

• For full-length windows, continue curtains onto the floor instead of leaving them hovering just above it. This gives a more luxurious feel and can help to overcome the problem of uneven floors or windows.

Type of fabric

• Almost any type of fabric can be used for these curtains. One advantage of corded tracks is that they allow the curtains to be pulled without being handled. This is useful for white curtains or curtains in fragile or antique fabrics that might become spoiled if pulled manually every day.

• Remember that large windows dominate a room so keep this in mind when choosing a fabric. An extremely bold pattern might be overpowering.

• Curtains of this type benefit from interlining. It makes the curtains more sumptuous and adds an insulating layer.

Options

• For additional interest, fit a tieback at each side to tuck the curtains behind. This gives shape to the way that the curtains frame the windows.

• Cover the lath and fascia in a different fabric from the curtains to make a feature of them. Or match the colour of the walls to make them blend in.

WHAT YOU WILL NEED

Main fabric for each curtain and to cover lath and fascia

Width
Finished width of curtain (see pp. 38–39), plus allowance for gathering of heading tape (see p. 40), plus 10 cm (4 in) for side hems

Length
Finished drop of curtain (see pp. 38–39), plus 25 cm (10 in) for top and base hems

Fabric for lath and fascia
Enough fabric to cover both the lath and fascia completely

Lining fabric for each curtain

Width
As for main fabric

Length
As for main fabric

Interlining fabric for each curtain

Width
As for main fabric

Length
As for main fabric, less 10 cm (4 in)

Accessories

Tape
2.5-cm (1-in) tape cut to width of fabric, plus 5 cm (2 in) for finishing ends

Brass curtain hooks
1 for every 10 cm (4 in) of pulled-up tape, plus 1 at each end

Track
Metal track that can be attached to the back of the fascia. If the track needs to be curved as here, this requires specialist tools and so it is advisable to seek professional help

Lath
5- x 2.5-cm (2- x 1-in) lath cut to fit inside the bay

Fascia
5-cm (2-in) deep fascia cut to the same length as the lath

Attaching the interlining

When making a large lined and interlined curtain, it is best to spread the fabric across the worktable and stitch a width of fabric at a time (see pp. 38 and 42–43). The entire base hem is pressed into place first, but then just stitch to the end of the first width. At this point you should lock in the interlining (see p. 44) to the main fabric (see Step 2), before continuing to the next width.

1 Follow the instructions on p. 45 to attach the interlining to the back of the curtain with a double lining hem at the base and mitred corners. Insert covered weights (see inset and p. 46) into the base hem at the corners and at each width.

2 As you work your way across the curtain, lock in (see p. 44) each width of interlining to the main fabric.

Attaching the lining

1 Take the contrast lining and turn and press a double 5-cm (2-in) hem along the base (see p. 46). Machine stitch the base hem in place.

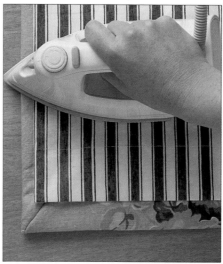

2 Lay the lining on the curtain, wrong sides together, turning under the edges at the side hem and press as shown. Position the lining so that it is about 2.5 cm (1 in) in from the edges of the curtain and pin in place.

3 Secure the lining fabric to the edge of the curtain at the left-hand side using slipstitch (see p. 44).

4 *Lock in the lining across the curtain at width and half-width positions (see p. 43).*

5 *Loosely secure the lining at the base hem at width and half-width intervals, using daisy chain stitch (see p. 45) as shown. Finally, secure the lining to the edge of the curtain at the right-hand side, as in Step 3, p. 78.*

Attaching the heading tape

1 *Mark the finished drop line at the top of the curtain on the wrong side and press over the raw edge about 5 cm (2 in).*

2 *Pin the tape across the top of the curtain so that it covers the raw edges of the curtain top and machine stitch the tape in place.*

3 *Secure one end of the tape following the instructions on p. 48 and pull up the strings of the heading tape until the curtain is gathered to its required width. Make sure that the fullness is evenly distributed across the width.*

4 *Knot the strings of the tape, rolling the surplus into a bow shape and stitch the strings to the tape (see inset). Cover the lath and fascia (see p. 56), attach the track and hang the curtains.*

LINED CURTAINS WITH DRAPE

BOLD COLOURS, combined in a classic arrangement, make these chenille curtains and slot-headed drape an eye-catching focal point for a room. The curtains have a pencil-pleat heading and are hung from a corded track that is fixed to the wall above the French windows and hidden behind the drape. They fall into soft undulating folds, which are held back by small metal pole finials attached to the frame of the doors.

The drape at the top slots over a pole made of the same material as the finials. Wide bands in a contrasting colour loop the drape into shape, making a scoop that, at its deepest, is about one-sixth of the overall drop of the curtains. The track and pole are fitted close together in the wall above the window, as the curtains do not need to be drawn open or closed.

Type of window

• Full-length curtains with a pelmet or drape need tall, elegant windows. Here, the arrangement created by the tieback curtains and the scoop of the drape is contained within the shape of the French windows.

• These curtains and drape would also suit a single window or door or a matching pair of windows.

Type of fabric

• For a strong but simple look, use plain fabrics, with a striking colour contrast between the drape and the curtains.
• Velvets, chenilles or heavy wools are perfect for these curtains. They have the right texture and weight to drape well and retain their shape.
• Create an even more dramatic effect with a wide black and white stripe for the curtain and a narrower stripe for the drape, with contrast bands of burgundy or emerald.

Options

• Use a diagonal stripe or tapestry strip for the bands to add interest.
• For a more subtle arrangement, make both curtains and drape in one fabric, with just the bands at the top in a contrasting colour.
• Move the contrast bands to the centre to give a different shape to the base of the drape.

WHAT YOU WILL NEED: CURTAIN

Main fabric for each curtain

Width
Finished width of curtain (see pp. 38–39), plus allowance for gathering of taped heading (see p. 40), plus 10 cm (4 in) for side hems

Length
Finished drop of curtain (see pp. 38–39), plus 25 cm (10 in) for top and base hems

Lining fabric for each curtain

Width
As for main fabric

Length
As for main fabric, less 10 cm (4 in)

Accessories

7.5-cm (3-in) tape
Width of fabric, plus 5 cm (2 in) for turning

Brass curtain hooks
1 for every 10 cm (4 in) of pulled-up tape, plus 1 at each end

Covered curtain weights
1 for each corner, plus 1 for each width

Corded track
Finished width of curtain

WHAT YOU WILL NEED: DRAPE

Fabric for drape

Width
Finished width of drape, plus 8 cm (3 in) for hems

Length
Finished drop of drape (about one-sixth of total drop of curtains), plus 31 cm (12 ¼ in) for hems, plus depth needed for the slot according to the size of pole (see p. 40)

Fabric for each band and piping

Width
Twice finished width of band, plus 2 cm (¾ in) for seams. The width of band shown here is 6 cm (2¼ in)

Length
The length required, plus 4 cm (1½ in) for seams. The length of band shown here is 25 cm (10 in)

Piping
Joined 5-cm (2-in) wide bias-cut strips (see p. 47) the finished width of the drape, plus 4 cm (1½ in) for turning in raw ends

Accessories

Piping cord
Finished width of drape

Pole
Metal pole with finials the width of the window, plus at least 20 cm (8 in). 2 extra finials to act as tiebacks for the curtains

Making the curtain

1 *On the wrong side of the curtain, press over single 5-cm (2-in) side hems and a double 10-cm (4-in) base hem (see p. 46 for information on base hems).*

2 *Fold back the side hems and fold back the base hem once. Secure the raw edge of the base hem with herringbone stitch (see p. 44).*

3 *Fold over the corner of the hem diagonally as shown, so that the pressed line of the side hem lines up with herringboned edge of the base hem. Insert a covered weight in what will be the finished corner and stitch in place.*

4 *Fold up the base hem again over the covered weight. Pin the base hem in place.*

Covered weight

Double base hem pinned in place

5 *Fold and press the side hem in again, forming a neat mitred corner and pin it in place. Repeat Steps 3 to 5 to mitre the corner at the other side of the curtain and then secure the side hems with herringbone stitch and the mitred corners and top of the base hem with slipstitch (see p. 44) as shown.*

Side hem folded in

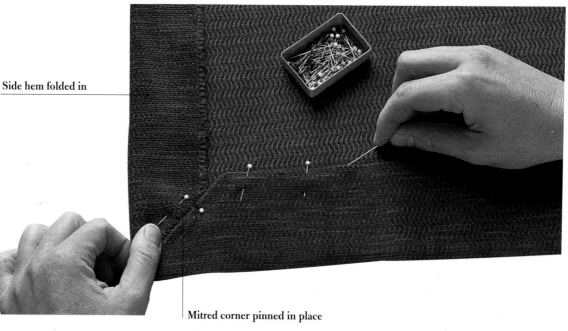

Mitred corner pinned in place

Attaching the lining

1 *Fold and machine stitch a double 5-cm (2-in) base hem on the lining fabric (see p. 46).*

2 *Lay the lining on the back of the curtain, wrong sides together, so that it covers the curtain's stitched base and side hems. Press under the lining's raw edges by 2.5 cm (1 in) at the sides and slip-stitch it to the sides of the curtain as shown.*

3 *Fold back the lining at the base and loosely secure the top of the lining base hem to the top of the curtain base hem using daisy chain stitch (see p. 45). Secure it at width and half-width intervals (see p. 43).*

Finishing the curtain

1 *Measure the finished drop from the base of the curtain and mark the finished drop line with pins at the top of the curtain on the wrong side. Press over the raw edges 5 cm (2 in) at the top (see inset) and remove pins.*

2 *Pin the heading tape to the top of the curtain and machine stitch top and bottom. Secure one end of tape by knotting the strings, folding tape under and stitching across (see p. 48). This secures the strings and prevents them from unraveling.*

3 *Pull up the tape until the curtain is gathered to its finished width. Make sure that the gathering is evenly distributed across the width. Knot the strings of the tape.*

4 *Roll surplus strings up into a bow shape. Stitch the rolled up strings firmly to heading tape. Repeat to make second curtain, insert hooks (see p. 48) and hang on track (see p. 53).*

Making the bands for the drape

Fabric folded in half lenghwise | Machine stitch along pinned edge

Underside of band turned right side out | Seam pressed flat

1 *To make the two contrast bands, fold the fabric in half lengthwise, right sides together and pin along the length 1 cm (⅜ in) in from the edge. Machine stitch along pin line.*

2 *Turn the fabric right side out and press so that seam lies in the centre of the underside. Repeat to make the other band.*

Making the drape

1 *Pin double 2-cm (¾-in) hems along the sides and base of the fabric for the drape. Machine stitch the hems in place.*

2 *Measure, from the top of the fabric for the drape, the depth needed for the slot (see p. 40) and cut off this fabric. Put it aside until Step 1 of Attaching the slot head to the drape, p. 85.*

20 cm (8 in)

3 *Lay the rest of the fabric for the drape right side up and position the two bands on top of it, aligning the bands' raw edges with the top of the drape section and about 20 cm (8 in) in from each edge. Pin in place.*

4 *Place the made-up piping (see p. 47) along the top of the drape section. Machine stitch the piping to the drape, sewing over the contrast bands to secure them.*

Attaching the slot head to the drape

1 *Place the slot fabric (see Step 2 of Making the drape, p. 84) along top of the drape, right sides together. Machine stitch the slot to the drape, stitching over the bands and the edges of the piping.*

2 *Open out the slot and mark the fold line, which will be the top of the drape, with pins.*

3 *Press over the slot section to the wrong side of the drape along the fold line, turning under the raw edge by 2 cm (³/₄ in).*

4 *Pin the slot in place so that it covers the seam as shown and secure it with slipstitch.*

5 *Take each band around to the back of the drape, gathering the drape up at the same time. When the band is the required length, turn in the raw edge and slipstitch the end of the band to the back of the drape, beneath the slot.*

6 *Hang the curtain from a track and slot the drape onto a pole fitted close to the track. The two have to be close together for the arrangement to work. Before attaching the tiebacks for the curtains (see below), experiment by holding the curtain back by hand to see at what height the draping works to best effect.*

STRIPED CURTAINS

THESE EYE-CATCHING single curtains are made from strips of fabric sewn together, with alternating dark blue and dark green strips set between strips of cream. Across the top they have a wide slot heading made of the same fabrics, but stitched together in a contrasting order. Edging each curtain and dividing the slot at the top from the main section, is a length of piping in brilliant emerald green. This catches the light and contrasts with the matt surface of the rest of the fabric.

These curtains are intended to hang simply from their poles as flat panels. Rather than being drawn, chunky cream rope and tassel tiebacks hold the curtains in shape and keep them off the windows.

Type of window

• These curtains work well on either tall or short windows. Bear in mind that they do not draw across the top.
• It is important that single curtains look deliberate, not accidental. Fill the spaces between a pair of windows with pictures and make a feature of the way the curtains are hung with tiebacks.

Type of fabric

• The fabric used here is a crisp, stiff cotton. It is glazed but used on the reverse side. Plain colours, such as these, look best, but they can be either close to each other in tone or contrasting in colour for a dramatic effect.
• Fabrics for the strips need to be of the same type or there is a danger of tension and stretching. Seams must stay flat inside the curtains, so avoid fabric that is bulky or that may fray.

Options

• For an understated, minimalist look, try using two fabrics that are close in colour, such as creams or off-white cottons or linens.
• For a less bold look, alter the width of stripe, but remember that the narrower the stripes, the more work there is. Try offsetting the main stripes with colours other than cream.

WHAT YOU WILL NEED

Main fabric for each curtain and slot heading

To calculate amount of stripes needed for each curtain, divide finished width of curtain by finished width of each stripe – here, 100 cm (40 in) divided by 10 cm (4 in), making 10 stripes

Width for curtain

For each stripe: finished width of curtain (see pp. 38–39), divided by amount of stripes, plus 4 cm (1½ in) for side hems

Length for curtain

For each stripe: finished drop of curtain (see pp. 38–39), minus finished drop of slot heading, plus 22 cm (8¾ in) for base hem and top seam

Width for slot heading

For each stripe: finished width of curtain, divided by amount of stripes, plus 4 cm (1½ in) for side hems

Length for slot heading

For each stripe: twice the finished drop of slot heading (see p. 40), plus 4 cm (1½ in) for hems. The slot heading on this curtain has a drop of 25 cm (10 in)

Lining and piping fabric for each curtain

Width for lining

Finished width of curtain, plus 2.5 cm (1in) for side hems

Length for lining

Finished drop of curtain, plus twice finished drop of slot heading, plus 12 cm (4¾ in) for base hem and top seams

Piping fabric

Joined 5-cm (2-in) bias-cut strips (see p. 47): 1 piece finished width of curtain, plus twice the finished drop; 2 pieces each finished drop of slot heading, plus 2 cm (¾ in)

Accessories

Piping cord

As for piping fabric

Pole

Width of the window frame, plus however much you want it to extend either side (see p. 52)

Tiebacks

1 for each curtain

Making the curtain

1 *Lay out the cut strips for the first curtain in the desired order and, with right sides together and 2-cm (¾-in) seams, machine stitch each strip to the next along their long edges to make the main curtain.*

2 *Fold over the seams to the centre of each dark stripe so they do not show through the lighter stripes and press.*

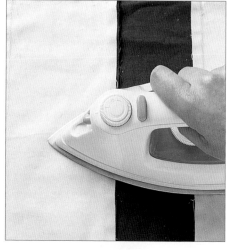

3 *Fold over a double 10-cm (4-in) hem at the base of the curtain and press (see p. 46 for more details on base hems).*

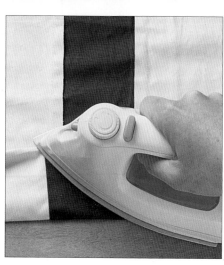

4 *Pin the hem in place and secure it with herringbone stitch (see p. 44). Repeat Steps 1 and 2 to make the slot heading, joining strips so the dark strips on the slot line up with the light ones on the main curtain.*

Attaching the piping and slot

1 *With curtain right side up, pin and machine stitch made-up piping (see p. 47) to both sides of curtain and across top. Attach piping to sides only of slot heading.*

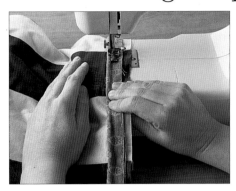

2 *Place the slot heading over piping at top of curtain, right sides together. Machine stitch beside piping line, allowing a 2-cm (¾-in) seam.*

Main curtain

Slot heading

Finishing the curtain

1 *Having pressed and stitched a double 5-cm (2-in) base hem on lining, place lining on back of curtain, pressing under raw edges close to piping. Slipstitch (see p. 44) in place along base and sides.*

2 *At the top of the curtain, fold the heading section over to make the slot. Press under the raw edge.*

3 *Secure the lower edge of the slot heading section with slip-stitch. Repeat the whole process to make the second curtain. Put up the poles and hang the curtains (see p. 52).*

VARIATION ON STRIPED CURTAIN

This curtain demonstrates a wonderfully creative use of fabric. Long strips, made up of squares and rectangles of coloured silk, are inset between sections of green velvet. The effect resembles a stylish patchwork and has a far less formal feel than the regimented stripes of the main project.

CURTAIN WITH SELF-PELMET

A WINDOW IN THE CORNER of a landing can be difficult to curtain successfully. This single self-pelmet curtain, set into the corner on one side and balanced visually by furniture and a wall light on the other, provides an elegant solution.

The fringed self-pelmet makes the curtain smart without being overly formal. Long goblet pleats are set into the top of the curtain, which has been folded down to give the impression of being a separate pelmet. The fringe, which is hand-sewn to the base of the self-pelmet, adds texture and helps define the two sections of the curtain.

Type of window

• This type of curtain looks best on tall windows that are longer than they are wide.
• If space permits, fit the pole from which the curtain hangs above the window. This has the effect of lengthening the curtain and uses the space above the window. The width of the heading should not extend beyond the window frame and the curtain should hang to the floor.

Type of fabric

• Damasks, brocades and tapestries would be excellent fabrics for this curtain, which lends itself to period settings.

While these may be first choices, this curtain could be made in almost any kind of fabric.
• Choose a fringe and tieback that complement the main fabric colour rather than contrasting with it. Fringes can be dyed to match fabrics if necessary.
• If you are using a lighter fabric you can add interlining (see p. 46), but with heavy fabrics, such as the one used here, this is probably not necessary.

Options

• Make a fabric skirt to hang in front at the top of the curtain. The two are held together by one line of eyelets through which a pole can thread. Add a border to the skirt to give definition.
• Try a casual arrangement with fabric draped behind and over a pole to look like a full-length curtain with a short pelmet drape above.
• Dispense with the self-pelmet and go for a simpler approach with no fringe.
• Double the impact by making two identical curtains and using them on a pair of matching windows. Tie one back to the right and one to the left to give an overall symmetrical effect. You could even use this style on a row of three windows, tying them all back in the same direction.

—— WHAT YOU WILL NEED ——

Main fabric for curtain

Width

Finished width of curtain (see pp. 38–39), plus 18 cm (7 in) for each pleat (see p. 40), plus 10 cm (4 in) for side hems

Length

Finished drop of curtain (see pp. 38–39), plus 22 cm (8¾ in) for the top and base hems, plus twice the depth of the self-pelmet. The depth of the self-pelmet shown here is 25 cm (10 in)

Lining and fringe fabric for curtain

Width for lining

As for main fabric

Length for lining

As for main fabric, less 10 cm (4 in) per drop

Fringe

As cut width for main fabric, plus 4 cm (1½ in) for finishing raw ends

Accessories

Pin hooks

As number of pleats, plus 2

Curtain weights

2 for each width of fabric (see p. 43)

Pole

Width of window frame and with removable finials so that one end can be butted up right against the wall

Making the curtain

5-cm (2-in)
side hem

20-cm (8-in)
base hem

Crease of
side hem

Curtain
weight

Crease of
base hem

1 *Place the main fabric right side down and press over 5-cm (2-in) hems on each side. Fold over a 20-cm (8-in) hem at the base of the curtain and press.*

2 *Open the pressed hems. Fold in each corner of the base hem so that the diagonal fold is at the point where the side and base creases align and press in place. Sew a curtain weight in each corner of the base hem. (See p. 46 for more details on curtain weights.)*

Double hem
at base

Mitred
corner

3 *Press the base hem over 10 cm (4 in) twice to form a double 10-cm (4-in) hem. Fold the side hem in to form a neat mitred corner. Press and secure the corner with slipstitch (see p. 44). Repeat on the other corner of the base hem.*

4 *Secure both of the side hems of the curtain with herringbone stitch (see p. 44).*

5 *Once both side hems are stitched in place, secure the base hem of the curtain with slipstitch.*

Attaching the lining

Edge of lining 2 cm (¾ in) in from edge of curtain

5-cm (2-in) hem along the base

1 *Having machine stitched a 5-cm (2-in) hem along the base, press over 5-cm (2-in) hems on each side of the lining. Position the lining on the curtain, wrong sides together, with edges of the lining 2 cm (¾ in) in from edges of the curtain. Pin in place and slipstitch (see p. 44) sides of lining to the fabric.*

2 *Secure the underside of the base hem of the lining to the base hem of the curtain by hand, using daisy chain stitch (see p. 45).*

Making the self-pelmet

1 *At the top of the curtain, press over the lining and fabric to make a 2-cm (¾-in) hem on the lining side of the curtain.*

2 *Fold the curtain over to the right side to twice the depth of the finished self-pelmet. Fold up again so that the edge with the pressed hem aligns with the fold at the top of the curtain. Pin in place.*

3 *Secure the top of the curtain with slipstitch. Take care to stitch through all layers of the curtain and self-pelmet so the folded section stays in place.*

4 *Lay the length of fringe along the unstitched folded edge of the self-pelmet. Stitch the fringe in place along the fold so that it hangs below the pelmet. Stitch the fringe to the pelmet fold only, not through all layers of fabric.*

5 *Pin the ends of the pelmet section in place, tucking in the raw ends of the fringe as you do so. Secure the ends of the pelmet with slipstitch (see p. 44).*

Making up the goblet pleats

Spacing your pleats

To work out how much space you have between each pleat, first subtract 20 cm (8 in) from the curtain's width to allow for 10 cm (4 in) of unpleated area at each edge. Multiply the amount of pleats you want by 18 cm (7 in) and also subtract this total from the width. Finally, divide the resulting sum by the amount of spaces you need between the pleats (the amount of pleats minus 1).

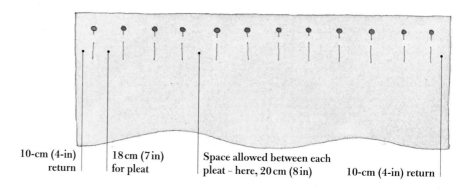

10-cm (4-in) return

18 cm (7 in) for pleat

Space allowed between each pleat – here, 20 cm (8 in)

10-cm (4-in) return

Pin 10 cm (4 in) from edge

Pin another 18 cm (7 in) from edge

1 *Measure 10 cm (4 in) in from one edge and mark with a pin. Measure and mark another 18 cm (7 in) for the first pleat and then do the same for the amount of space to be left between each pleat (see diagram above). Continue to measure and mark alternately the allowance for the pleats and for the space in between until, after the last pleat, you are 10 cm (4 in) from the other side.*

2 *To make a pleat, fold back the first pin to meet the second pin, wrong sides together (see inset). Machine stitch along the line of the pins through all layers down to and over the top of the fringe.*

3 *Fold back the third pin to meet the fourth and repeat the process until you have folded and stitched all of the pleats. Open them out.*

4 *On the back of the curtain, insert a pin hook on the stitched line of each pleat and at each end beyond the pleats. Hang the curtain (see p. 52) and attach the tieback.*

VARIATIONS ON CURTAIN WITH SELF-PELMET

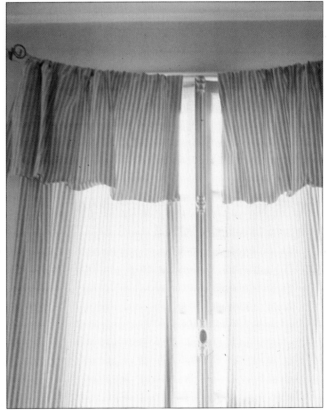

Curtain with self-pelmet, border and ties
This pelmet is simply an extra length of fabric that was added to the top of the finished drop and folded forwards so that it falls in front of the curtain. The curtain is held to the pole by ties attached to the top (see p. 17). A perimeter border, made in the same contrasting fabric as the ties, adds definition.

Unsewn curtains with self-pelmet
These curtains are simplicity itself and show how effectively fabric can be used with little or no sewing. The two pieces of striped fabric were cut to the right width and length and then slung over a curtain wire. The folded section at the top of each curtain creates a practical and visual balance.

PLAIN ROMAN BLIND

THE APPEAL OF ROMAN BLINDS lies in their simplicity and the economical use they make of both fabric and window space. They are little more than panels of fabric that lie flat against the window when down and have a simple cording mechanism that allows them to be raised in a series of simple folds.

The cording mechanism works with the help of a number of thin wooden battens called dowel rods. Rods are attached to the lining and run horizontally across the back of the blind at regular intervals. The blind is supported on a lath hung across the top of the window, and the cord runs up through a series of rings attached to the rods in the centre and at each side of the blind up to the lath at the top. The cords then run across to one side of the blind where they are secured to a drop weight.

Type of window

• Roman blinds suit almost any type of window and many different styles of room. This type of blind fits neatly within or close to the framed shape of the window and does not detract from the window's own architectural or decorative features.

• They are particularly useful where there is no room for curtains to hang at either side of a window and where you want a clean, uncluttered look.

• This style of blind is not suitable for windows more than 1.5 m (5 ft) wide. Blinds any wider than this are difficult to manoeuvre, but you can get around this by using a row of blinds.

Type of fabric

• Follow the blind's strong, vertical shape and choose simple stripes or checks or a strong pattern that is not lost when the blind is folded up. Avoid anything that is too fussy or busy.

• Choose a fabric that will keep its shape when folded. Crisp cottons are easiest to work with, but heavy wool tartan or even fine muslin also work well.

Options

• A blind made in a strong colour or pattern stands out, especially against paler walls. If the blind is made in a plain fabric similar in colour to the surrounding walls, it merges and takes on an architectural quality.

• To add interest at the top of the blind, attach a strip of the same or contrasting fabric to the lath at the top to make a false pelmet.

• Add borders or insets in contrasting colours or fabrics to give more interest or pick up a colour that appears elsewhere in the room.

WHAT YOU WILL NEED

Main fabric for blind

Width
*Finished width of blind (see pp. 38–39),
plus 10 cm (4 in) for side hems*

Length
*Finished drop of blind (see pp. 38–39),
plus 5 cm (2 in) for the base hem, plus 25 cm
(10 in) for attaching the top to the lath*

Lining fabric for blind
and rod pockets

Width for lining
As for main fabric

Length for lining
As for main fabric

Width for each rod pocket
12 cm (4¾ in)

Length for each rod pocket
Finished width of blind, plus 4 cm (1½ in)

Accessories

Dowel rods
*As number of rod pockets cut to the
finished width of blind*

Lath
*5- x 2.5-cm (2- x 1-in) timber lath cut to the
finished width of blind*

Brass rings
As number of rod pockets, multiplied by 3

Screw eyes
As number of rows of rings, plus 1

Polyester cord
*Enough for twice the drop of the blind,
plus the width, multiplied by the number
of rows of rings (see p. 54)*

Brass drop weight and cleat

Making the blind

1 *Lay the fabric for the blind right side down. Fold over and press 5-cm (2-in) hems down each side and at the base. Make sure that the corners are square.*

Square corner

2 *Unfold the pressed hems and turn in each corner so that the diagonal fold is at the point where side and base creases intersect. Press the corners.*

Crease along side

Crease along base

3 *Turn the side and base hems in again so that the folds meet. Stitch them together by hand, using slipstitch (see p. 44). Repeat at the other corner.*

4 *Secure the sides and base hem of the blind with herringbone stitch (see p. 44).*

5 *Press 5-cm (2-in) hems on the side and base of the lining. Pin and slipstitch it onto the blind, wrong sides together, so that about 1cm (⅜ in) of the blind's hem shows beyond the lining.*

Making the rod pockets

1 *Take the fabric for one rod pocket and fold it in half lengthwise, wrong sides together. Turn over the long raw edges 1cm (⅜ in) to form a hem and press.*

2 *Turn over the same long edge by 1cm (⅜ in) again to form a double hem. Press and machine stitch the double hem in place.*

3 *At one end, fold the raw edges over twice to form a double 1-cm (⅜-in) hem. Press and machine stitch this hem in place as well. Repeat to make other pockets.*

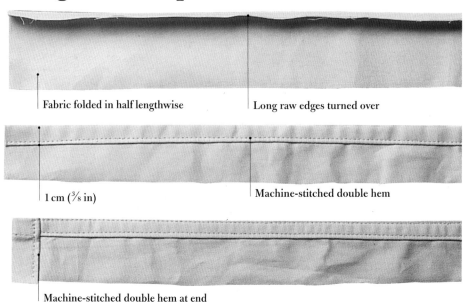

Fabric folded in half lengthwise | Long raw edges turned over

1 cm (⅜ in) | Machine-stitched double hem

Machine-stitched double hem at end

4 *Mark the position of the rod pockets (see p. 54) onto the back of the blind in pencil. Pin each pocket into place along its folded edge to align with the pencil marks.*

Position marked in pencil

5 *Machine stitch the pocket in place through all layers, keeping close to the folded edge.*

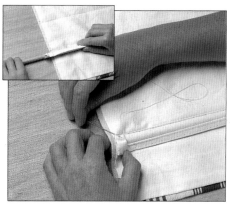

6 *After inserting a dowel rod into the pocket (see inset), finish the open end by turning in a double 1-cm (⅜-in) hem and securing with slipstitch. Repeat to make remaining pockets.*

Cording the blind

Screw eye

Lath

Cord

Brass ring

Brass drop weight

Rod pocket with rod inside

1 *Couch stitch (see p. 45) three brass rings to each pocket – one at each end, just in from the side, and one in the centre (see diagram).*

2 *Fix the lath to the top of the blind following the instructions on p. 55.*

3 *Check the fabric is hanging completely straight and screw the screw eyes through the fabric into the lath on the back side. Attach one in line with each of the rows of brass rings and attach another one just in from the edge of the lath on the side where the pull strings will be (see pp. 54–55).*

4 *Tie one length of white cord to the ring in the bottom left-hand corner. Thread it up through the row of rings and the screw eye at the top and then along the top through the remaining screw eyes. Leave a loose end of cord the same length as the blind. Take cords through the other rows of rings in the same way (see diagram and p. 54).*

5 *With the blind unfolded, make sure that all the cords are straight and that all the loose ends are the same length. Thread the loose ends of the cords through a brass drop weight and secure with a tight knot so they do not slip through. Trim the ends of the cords and fix the blind in position (see pp. 56–57).*

ROLLED BLIND WITH TIES

THE BEAUTY OF THIS elegant blind lies in its simplicity. It uses fabric in its most unstructured form, falling naturally from its support. Since it does not have a cording system, this blind is decorative rather than functional. To operate it, you simply roll up the lower part of the blind to the desired position from the base and then hold it in place with ties, which are made here in an attractive contrasting fabric.

The blind is made so that some of the front fabric is taken around to the back of the blind at its base. This ensures that no lining fabric is visible when the blind is rolled up. At the top of the blind is a simple slot or sleeve for the pole support.

Type of window

• This style of blind is excellent for a window that is not very attractive or that looks onto an unappealing view. The blind can be kept half-lowered, as here, held in place by the knotted ties.

• Tall rectangular sash or casement windows are suitable for this simple blind.

• There must be enough space above the window casement for a pole to be fitted so that the fabric falls outside and in front of the window.

• It is a useful blind for situations such as a staircase window, where the blind is decorative and does not need to be raised and lowered regularly.

Type of fabric

• The silk taffeta used here is the perfect fabric for this blind. It is not heavy, but stays in place when rolled up and shimmers against the light.

• Alternatively, use any fabric that keeps its shape when rolled. Since so much of the fabric is visible most of the time, a bold, large-scale pattern can be used successfully.

• The ties should provide a strong visual contrast, so choose the fabric accordingly. In this example, boldly coloured silk taffetas are used for both the blind and the ties, but the different scale of check and the strong colour contrast adds interest and drama to the finished look.

Options

• Instead of slotting the blind onto a pole, try hanging it with special clips that loop the pole and grip the fabric. Many types of decorative clips are available, but they are only strong enough to hold lightweight fabric such as silk taffeta (see variation on p. 103).

• For a more solid country look, use a bare wooden pole instead of the slender metal pole shown here. Or, paint a pole to match the fabric you choose for the blind or other colours in the room.

• Try making the blind and ties in strongly contrasting fabrics to create a different look. For example, use rough linen for the blind and make ties in velvet, or try a plain bleached sailcloth with hessian ties.

WHAT YOU WILL NEED

Main fabric for blind

Width

Finished width of blind (see pp. 38–39), plus 10 cm (4 in) for side hem allowances

Length

Finished drop of blind (see pp. 38–39), plus 50 cm (20 in) to go around to the back of the blind, plus 4 cm (1½ in) for hem allowances, plus allowance for slot at the top (see p. 41)

Lining fabric for blind

Width

As for main fabric

Length

As for main fabric, less 100 cm (40 in)

Accessories

Ties

For each tie, a 12-cm (4¾-in) wide strip twice the finished drop of the blind, plus 100 cm (40 in), plus 2 cm (¾ in) for hem allowances

Pole

At least 45 cm (18 in) wider than the window frame so that it extends at least 22.5 cm (9 in) on each side

Making the blind

1 *Place the main blind fabric and lining right sides together, aligning the raw edges along the sides and the base. Machine stitch along the base about 2 cm (¾ in) from the raw edges.*

2 *Open out fabric and lining and place flat, wrong side up. Press over 5-cm (2-in) hems on both sides of fabric and lining. Secure fabric hems only with herringbone stitch (see p. 44).*

Lining

Main fabric pulled around to lining side

Bottom of blind

3 *Bring lining over the main fabric, wrong sides together, matching raw edges at the top. This pulls about 50 cm (20 in) of the main fabric around to the lining side.*

4 *Pin the lining to the blind at each side and slipstitch (see p. 44) together. Continue down the sides of the blind, stitching the sections of fabric together.*

5 *Fold over the raw edges at the top of the blind 2 cm (¾ in) and press.*

6 *Press over the top again to form the slot for the pole. The size of the slot depends on the size of pole used. Check the pole first with a scrap of fabric to help you work out the slot size. Make the slot big enough to allow the pole to move freely.*

7 *Once the size of the slot is correct, machine stitch along the base of the hem of the slot.*

Making the ties

Tie folded in half lengthwise

Raw edge

Machine stitching along top

Back side of finished tie

Raw edges pressed and slipstitched

Seam running down centre of back side

1 Take fabric for one tie and fold in half lengthwise, right sides together. Machine stitch close to the raw edges on the open long side only. Turn the tie right side out. Press the seam so that it lies in the centre of the back side of the tie and will be hidden from sight when sewn to the blind. Press under raw edges at each end of the tie and slipstitch. Repeat to make the other tie.

2 Fold one tie in half widthwise. Stitch centre fold to top of the blind, 20 cm (8 in) from left edge, so one half falls to the front of the blind and the other to the back. Repeat with second tie and stitch 20 cm (8 in) from right edge. Put up the pole (see p. 52) and hang the blind and then roll up the fabric base to the required height and knot the ties.

VARIATION ON ROLLED BLIND WITH TIES

If the fabric of the blind is not too heavy – this silk taffeta is as light as could be – it can be held onto the pole with decorative clips. The clips, which are available in many different designs and finishes, loop over the pole and clip to the edge of the fabric. Make the blind without a slot to use in this way, or simply remove it from the pole and clip it up, as shown here. This makes a neat and simple change in the look and the stitch line of the slot is barely visible. The clips used here are metal and can be painted to tone with the fabric colour.

LINED PANEL BLIND

ALTHOUGH MADE IN a similar way to a Roman blind, this lined, slot-headed blind has a softer look – it does not have the series of rods and pockets that make the Roman blind so crisp and tailored. When pulled up, this blind falls into deep sculptural folds, which remain even when it is fully lowered.

To prevent the blind from pulling towards the centre, one rod is fixed near the base in a pocket running between the two rows of rings. This also helps to keep the sides of the blind vertical. The rows of rings on the back for the cording mechanism are set a little in from both edges to give the blind its 'tailed' sides. The deep contrast border along the base emphasises the scooped shape of the blind, while narrower borders give definition to the sides.

To give it greater impact, the blind is hung so that it extends above and to each side of the window. Chunky wooden finials and brass brackets attaching the pole to the wall add texture and visual interest.

Type of window

• Single windows with space around them in rooms, halls or stairways suit this kind of blind. Make sure there is enough room for the pole.

• The shape and dramatic style of this bordered blind make it best used on its own. It would not work well in combination with a curtain.

Type of fabric

• Use a fairly weighty fabric so the folds form without being too sharp or crisp. When raised, the blind should have a casual effect. Indian cottons, as shown here, chenilles and tartans are all excellent choices for this blind.

• For a more opulent blind, use shimmery velvets – try canary yellow borders on a deep olive green blind. Heavy, tactile fabrics give the blind a cosy look, but it could also be made in more summery fabrics.

Options

• Experiment with different types of finial to suit your room – wrought iron, glass or painted wood, for example. The pole itself is not visible once the blind is fitted, so the finials can be of different material.

• To alter the shape of the blind slightly, bring the rows of rings farther in from the edges. This will deepen the 'tails' and emphasise the shape of the blind still more. Make sure the central 'scoop' still covers the window.

WHAT YOU WILL NEED

Main fabric for blind

Width
Finished width of blind (see pp. 38–39), less the width of side borders, plus 4 cm (1½ in) for side hems

Length
Finished drop of blind (see pp. 38–39), less depth of base border, plus allowance for slot according to size of pole being used (see p. 41), plus 4 cm (1½ in) for top and base hems

Border fabric for blind

Width of side borders
Twice the finished border width, plus 4 cm (1½ in) for side hems. The width of the side borders shown here is 5 cm (2 in)

Length of side borders
Finished drop of blind, plus allowance for slot according to size of pole being used (see p. 41), plus 4 cm (1½ in) for hems

Width of base border
Finished border width, plus 4 cm (1½ in) for hems. The width of the base border shown here is 15 cm (6 in)

Length of base border
Width of blind, plus twice the cut width of side borders

Lining fabric for blind and rod pocket

Width for main lining
As for main fabric

Length
As for main fabric

Rod pocket
A 12-cm (4¾-in) wide strip of lining the width of the blind between the rings (see p. 54), plus 4 cm (1½ in) for seam allowances

Accessories

Brass rings
Finished drop of the blind, divided by 15 if working in centimetres or 6 if working in inches, multiplied by 2

Screw eyes
3

Dowel rod
Width of blind between rings

Polyester cord
Enough for twice the drop of the blind, plus the width, multiplied by the number of rows of rings (see p. 54)

Curtain pole
At least 30 cm (12 in) longer than the width of the window

Brass drop weight and cleat

Making the blind

1 *Pin and machine stitch the side border fabric strips to the sides of the main fabric, with right sides together.*

2 *Pin the base border in place, running it across the side borders, and machine stitch.*

3 *With blind right side down, press raw edges of seams at sides and base of the blind towards the borders.*

Side border folded in half to wrong side

Base border folded in with outer edges folded in diagonally

4 *Press the side borders in half over to the wrong side of the blind. At the base of the blind, fold the side borders in first and the base border over them. Fold and press under the outer edges of the base border diagonally, as shown, to finish neatly.*

5 *Secure the folded edges in place with slipstitch (see p. 44) and the side and base borders with herringbone stitch (see p. 44). Don't worry about the raw edges; they will be covered by the lining.*

6 *Place the lining on the back of the blind, wrong sides together. Tuck under raw edges and position as shown above, so that it covers the edges of the borders. Pin and slipstitch the lining in place along sides and base of the blind.*

7 *Press over a 2-cm (¾-in) hem at the top of the blind, tucking under the raw edges of the fabric and lining as you go. Pin the hem in place at the top and secure with slipstitch.*

8 *Mark with pins the line where the slot will be folded over. This fold line will be the top of the finished blind.*

9 *Fold the top of the blind over at the marked line to make the slot. Press the slot section in place.*

10 *Pin the slot in place on the wrong side of the blind and slipstitch along the base to secure.*

Making the rod pocket and cording the blind

1 *Attach the rings to the back of the blind. Make two vertical rows, each set in 10 cm (4 in) from the sides of the blind. Set the lowest ring in each row 15 cm (6 in) above the top of the base border. Set the remaining rings about 15 cm (6 in) apart. Calculate the position of the rings upwards from the lowest ring, with the highest ring being at least 20 cm (8 in) from the top.*

Slot heading

Screw eyes attached to top of window frame

Side border

Cords

Brass ring

Rod pocket with rod inside

Brass drop weight

Base border

2 *Make the rod pocket (see Steps 1–3, p. 98) and pin and stitch it to the back of the blind just above the base of the lining. Insert the dowel rod into the pocket.*

3 *Finish the open end of the rod pocket by turning in a double 1-cm (³⁄₈-in) hem and securing with slipstitch. When stitched, both ends should align vertically with the rows of rings 10 cm (4 in) in from either side of the blind.*

4 *Thread a length of cord through each of the rows of rings at the back of the blind (see p. 54). Once the blind is up on its pole, thread the cords through screw eyes mounted in the window frame and into a drop weight.*

UNLINED BLIND WITH BORDERS

ALTHOUGH SIMILAR IN CONSTRUCTION to the Roman blind (see p. 96), this blind has a very different look. It has a cording mechanism that you use to raise and lower it, but the mechanism only operates down the sides and there are no rods across the back. When the blind is pulled up, its sides are left to swing in and an attractive scooped shape is created along the base.

The blind is also unlined, which lets the fabric fold more freely and allows light through during the day, and it has a crisp border that gives the edges added definition.

Type of window

• This blind works well on windows that are flat to the wall, provided there is sufficient space on either side, or on recessed windows where the blind is face-fixed. It is suited equally well to portrait windows and square-shaped windows, as well as windows set side by side.
• This blind is useful for windows with unappealing views since, being unlined, it still allows light in when it is lowered. If you wish to block out all light while sleeping, fit a blackout roller blind behind it.

Type of fabric

• If you are making a small blind, avoid large patterns. Use stripes, checks or small, pretty patterns. Alternatively, you can use strong plain colours for the main section and small patterns for the borders. Vary the border width, if necessary, to follow the width of a stripe or other pattern.
• Reversible fabrics, or fabrics with a definite front and back so the blind looks attractive from the outside, are also suitable.
• Avoid heavy fabrics, such as velvets and brocades, which would pull the sides of the blind in too much.

Options

• Two rows of rings set in from the sides of the blind give the scooped effect. If you add a central row of rings, the blind lifts in the centre and alters the shape of the base.
• Deepen the border along the base and remove the side borders to create a different effect and emphasise the shape of the blind.
• Make a slot along the top of the blind and hang it from a pole.

——— WHAT YOU WILL NEED ———

Main fabric for blind

Width
Finished width of blind (see pp. 38–39), less twice the width of the border, plus 4 cm (1½ in) for seam allowances

Length
Finished drop of blind (see pp. 38–39), plus 2 cm (¾ in) for the base hem, plus 25 cm (10 in) for attaching the top to the lath

Border fabric for blind

Side (vertical) borders
2 borders, each the cut drop of the blind by twice the finished border width, plus 4 cm (1½ in) for seam allowances. The width of the border shown here is 5 cm (2 in)

Base (horizontal) border
The cut width of the blind, plus twice the cut width of a side border by the finished border width, plus 4 cm (1½ in) for seam allowances

Accessories

Lath
5- x 2.5-cm (2- x 1-in) timber lath cut to the finished width of blind

Brass rings
Finished drop of the blind, divided by 15 if working in centimetres or 6 if working in inches, multiplied by 2

Screw eyes
3

Polyester cord
Enough for twice the drop of the blind, plus the width, multiplied by the number of rows of rings (see p. 54)

Brass drop weight and cleat

Making the blind

1 *Lay one border piece on top of the right-hand side of the fabric, with right sides together. Align and machine stitch it to the fabric 2 cm (¾ in) in from the edge. Repeat with left-hand side and then attach the base border, running the stitching across the side borders.*

2 *Place the blind right side down and press the raw edges of the seams toward the borders.*

3 *With right sides still down, fold over the raw edges of both the side borders and the base border of the blind by 2 cm (¾ in) and press.*

4 *Fold the side borders in, just covering the seam where the border is attached to the main fabric. Press and pin.*

Side border

Base border

5 *Fold the base border in to where the side borders meet it, making a neat edge. Press and pin.*

6 *Slipstitch (see p. 44) the side borders and the base border to the main fabric on the wrong side and remove the pins.*

7 *Slipstitch the outer edges of the base border where it overlaps side borders. To fit the lath and screw eyes to the top of the blind, follow instructions on p. 55.*

Cording the blind

1 *Stitch the rings to the back of the blind. Make two vertical rows, each 10 cm (4 in) from the sides of the blind. Set the lowest ring just above the base border. Set the rest 15 cm (6 in) apart, working upward from the lowest ring.*

2 *Tie one length of cord to the lowest ring in the left hand row. Thread through the rings and through the screw eye at the top. Take another cord and repeat with the second row (see p. 54).*

3 *After checking that both loose ends are the same length, thread both cords through the brass drop weight and secure them with a strong knot. Trim the ends of the cord and fix the blind in position (see pp. 56–57).*

VARIATION ON UNLINED BLIND WITH BORDERS

Set in front of a tall, elegant window recess, this unlined blind is made of a beautiful toile de Jouy print in unusual colours. As well as having no borders, it has a slightly different cording mechanism, with a central cord in addition to the two side cords. This levels the base, making it appear more like a standard Roman blind, but the absence of rods keeps the blind informal. As the blind folds up, it creates a shallow scoop on each side of the centre, lending a hint of softness to the shape. The cording mechanism here incorporates a tape sewn through all layers. This creates a slight gathered effect that adds to the visual appeal.

INVERTED PLEAT BLIND

A SMART, TAILORED BLIND, this is essentially a panel divided by a central inverted pleat. Both the colourful pleat and the matching flat border across the top add definition to the blind. A length of curtain tape is fitted to the back of the pleat and pulled up to give the base of the blind a scooped shape.

Type of window

• This style of blind needs to be long to look its best and works well on tall, narrow windows. It suits being held within an elegant frame or recess.

• The blind looks good pulled up only part way, forming soft folds and leaving much of the window permanently covered with fabric. Consider using this style of blind on a window that is not an important natural light source or one that looks out onto an unattractive view that would be better concealed.

Type of fabric

• For the best effect, use two different but compatible fabrics, such as cottons of a similar weight. Because it creases so easily, linen is less suitable, unless you want a more casual 'crumpled' look.

• Chenille or wool fabrics give a softer, weightier look to this blind. Alternatively, sheer fabrics, even flimsy muslins, look stunning and let light through.

• Choose patterns that still work well when divided by the pleat. On the divided sections, the patterns must match perfectly where they meet.

• Floral patterns inspired by classical Italian damasks suit this blind. Use smaller patterns or plain fabrics for the contrast pleat and border.

Options

• Instead of fixing the blind to a lath, make the border into a slot or sleeve for a pole. Allow space around the shade, both for pole fittings and for maximum impact, and add decorative finials.

• Deepen the border across the top to emphasise the length of the blind. Add a line of covered piping or chunky cord between the border and the main section of the blind to add texture and further contrast.

WHAT YOU WILL NEED

Main fabric for blind

Width
Finished width of blind (see pp. 38–39), plus 10 cm (4 in) for side hems, plus 4 cm (1½ in) for seams for joining to central pleat. Once cut, the fabric is cut in half again lengthwise. If using patterned fabric allow extra (see p. 41) for making sure the pattern matches perfectly where they meet in the centre

Length
Finished drop of the blind (see pp. 38–39), plus 7 cm (2¾ in) for hems, plus 25 cm (10 in) for fullness in the base of the blind

Fabric for pleat and border

Width for pleat
Twice the fullness of the pleat (see p. 41), plus 4-cm (1½-in) seam allowances for joining to main blind fabric

Length for pleat
As for main fabric

Width for border
Finished width of blind, plus 4 cm (1½ in) for seams

Length for border
Depth of border, plus 2 cm (¾ in) for hems, plus 25 cm (10 in) for rolling around lath

Lining fabric for blind and border

Width for blind lining
Finished width of blind, plus twice the fullness of the pleat

Length for blind lining
As for main fabric

Width for border lining
As for border

Length for border lining
As for border

Accessories

Tape
2.5-cm (1-in) tape cut to finished drop of blind

Rings
Finished drop of the blind, divided by 15 if working in centimetres or 6 if working in inches, multiplied by 2

Lath
5- x 2.5-cm (2- x 1-in) timber lath cut to the finished width of blind

Screw eyes
3

Polyester cord
Enough for twice the drop of the blind, plus the width, multiplied by 2 (see p. 54)

Brass drop weight and cleat

Making the blind

1 *Pin and machine stitch the contrast pleat fabric to each section of the main fabric, right sides together, with 2-cm (³⁄₄-in) seams. You will then have one large piece, with the pleat fabric in the centre and the two sections of main fabric on either side.*

2 *Press the seams towards the pleat so that they will not show from the front when the blind is hung. If your main fabric is darker than the pleat fabric, press the seams the other way.*

Pressed line of side hem   Pressed line of base hem

Base hem pressed in

3 *With the fabric still right side down, press over 5-cm (2-in) hems at the sides and base of the fold. Unfold the pressed hems and fold and press in each corner diagonally, aligning the pressed lines of the hems.*

4 *Turn the base hem in again and then the side hem (see inset) so that the folds meet. Slipstitch (see p. 44) them together and then secure the base and side hems with herringbone stitch (see p. 44).*

5 *Place the lining on the blind fabric wrong sides together. Press over the raw edges and pin in place so that the edge of the lining is 1 cm (³⁄₈ in) in from the sides of the main fabric.*

6 *Slipstitch the lining in place on the back of the blind down both of the sides.*

7 *Take a length of 2.5-cm (1-in) tape and pin it down the centre of the pleat on the wrong side of the blind. Machine stitch the tape to the blind through all layers.*

Knot strings at top

8 *Keep the strings of the tape open at the bottom of the blind, but knot them securely at the top.*

9 *With the blind right side up, mark a line down the centre of the pleated section and fold the main fabric into this line to form the pleat. Pin and press the pleat into position.*

Attaching the border

1 *Place the border lining right side down and place the blind on top of it wrong side down, aligning the top of the blind with a long edge of the border lining. Then place the border fabric on top of the blind, right side down. The border lining and border will both extend 5 cm (2 in) on both sides of the blind.*

Border lining right side down

Border right side down

Main fabric wrong side down

2 *Pin the three layers together across the top with a 2-cm (¾-in) seam and machine stitch. Keep the folded pleat carefully in position. The stitching also secures the tape – make sure the knot is on the border side of the stitching line.*

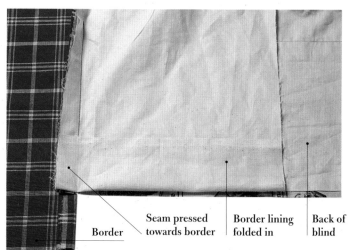

Border | Seam pressed towards border | Border lining folded in | Back of blind

3 *With the blind right side down, bring out the border from underneath it. Fold in the lining on both sides so that it aligns with the edge of the blind and press the seam towards the border.*

Border folded in

4 *Fold in border on each side in the same way as the lining so that it also aligns with edge of blind and press.*

5 *Fold border lining up so that it is lying on top of border, wrong sides together and slipstitch the sides together.*

Cording the blind

1 *Attach rings to back of blind in two vertical rows, each 10 cm (4 in) from sides of blind. Set lowest one in each row 5 cm (2 in) from base of blind. Set each ring about 30 cm (12 in) above the other. Spacing will vary with drop of blind but should not be less than this. Calculate upwards from lowest ring.*

2 *Attach the lath and screw eyes to the top of the blind (see p. 55) and thread a length of cord through each row of rings, through the screw eyes and into a brass drop weight (see p. 54).*

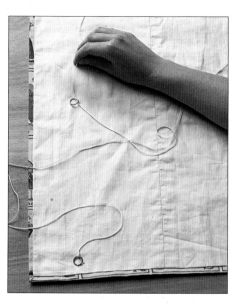

Pulling up the tape

1 *Pull on the central tape to give some fullness at the base of the blind. The amount will depend on individual taste, but on average, pull up by 20–25 cm (8–10 in).*

2 *Knot the tape cords together to keep them from unravelling. Hand-sew the knot to the back of the blind so that it does not show from the front and hang the blind (see p. 57).*

VARIATION ON INVERTED PLEAT BLIND

Instead of having just one central pleat, this blind has three, dividing it into four flat sections. The cording mechanism – one row of rings in the middle and one on each side – pulls the blind up into two 'scoops'. The pleats are similar to tucks and not very full. They catch the light, creating long thin shadows on the surface of the blind. Clever shaping at the top of the blind adds an elegance offset by the black painted moulding.

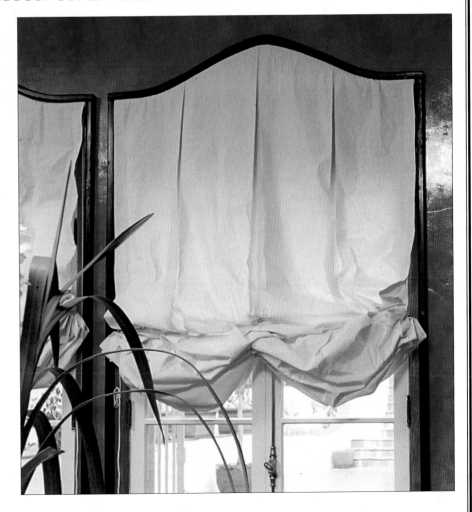

LINED AND PLEATED BLIND

I NVERTED PLEATS, evenly spaced across the width, emphasize the strong, clean lines of this blind and add fullness and form along the base. Cording is threaded through rows of rings set directly behind each pleat, so that soft folds form between the pleats as the blind is pulled up. This style of blind should be fitted to a lath, not hung from a pole, but it may be placed inside or outside a window recess.

Type of window

• This blind is best for windows with a horizontal shape, such as the example shown here. It adds softness to this type of featureless, deep-recessed casement.
• Avoid long portrait windows for this blind. The inverted pleats make a lot of fabric and a long blind would be difficult to raise and lower.
• If a window has vertical bars, use them as a guide for positioning the pleats, but do not follow them too rigidly. The blind looks better with some asymmetry.

Type of fabric

• You can use almost any fabric for this blind, but those that emphasise the shape, such as strong plain colours, stripes or checks are better than fabrics with busy overall patterns. The classic striped fabric used here provides just enough pattern and colour, without interfering with the sculptured shape of the blind.
• Crisp cotton and lightweight canvas both pleat well and are not too bulky when pulled up.
• Beware of fabrics with a pattern across the width for this blind. Ensure that any pattern chosen still works when the pleats are formed.
• For added interest, try using a contrast lining in a darker colour than the main fabric. Some diffused colour will show through when light shines through the blind.

Options

• Sew a fringe across the base of the blind to add texture and interest (see p. 29), but keep the fringe in style with the fabric and surroundings. On the blind shown here, for example, a chunky jute fringe would be more suitable than an ornate silky style with delicate tassels.
• To add depth and contrast, try making the pleats in a different fabric from the main blind.

WHAT YOU WILL NEED

Main fabric for blind

Width

Finished width of blind (see pp. 38–39), plus 10 cm (4 in) for the side hems, plus amount for each pleat (see p. 41 for calculating pleats), plus 10 cm (4 in) for returns

Length

Finished drop of blind (see pp. 38–39), plus 5 cm (2 in) for the base hem, plus 25 cm (10 in) for fullness at the base of the blind, plus 5 cm (2 in) for attaching the top to the lath

Lining fabric for blind

Width

As for main fabric, minus 10 cm (4 in)

Length

As for main fabric, minus 5 cm (2 in)

For covering lath

Enough fabric to cover the lath completely including the ends (see p. 55)

Accessories

Brass rings

Finished drop of blind, divided by 15 if working in centimetres or 6 if working in inches, multiplied by number of pleats plus 2

Lath

5- x 2.5-cm (2- x 1-in) timber lath cut to finished width of blind and covered with lining fabric (see p. 56)

Screw eyes

As number of pleats, plus 3

Polyester cord

Twice drop of blind plus width, multiplied by the number of pleats plus 2 (see p. 54)

Brass drop weight and cleat

Making the blind

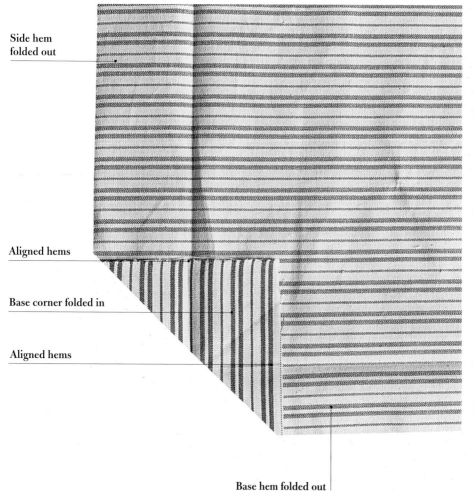

Side hem folded out

Aligned hems

Base corner folded in

Aligned hems

Base hem folded out

2 *Press the base and side hems back into place, making mitred corners. Make sure that the pattern matches up neatly where the side and base hems meet. Pin the corners in place.*

1 *With right side down, press over a single 5-cm (2-in) hem down both sides of the main fabric and along the base. Fold the side and base hems back out and fold in each base corner diagonally, aligning the pressed lines of the hems as shown.*

3 *Secure the side and base hems of the blind with herringbone stitch (see p. 44) and the mitred corners with slipstitch (see p. 44).*

Attaching the lining

1 *Place the lining fabric onto the back of the blind, wrong sides together. Fold under the raw edges of the lining along the bottom and sides so that it is about 1 cm (⅜ in) in from the edges of the blind. Press and pin it in place.*

2 *If you are making a blind as wide as the one here – finished width of 183 cm (72 in) – lock in the lining (see p. 44) across the blind at width and half-width intervals (see p. 43).*

3 *Slipstitch the lining in place along the sides and the base of the blind. Leave the top open.*

Making the pleats

1 *To mark the position of the pleats, measure from one edge the width between each pleat plus 5 cm (2 in) for the return and mark with a vertical line of pins. Here, the width between each pleat is 45 cm (18 in).*

2 *Measure from there the amount allowed for a pleat (see p. 41) and mark with a vertical line of pins. Here, 15 cm (6 in) is allowed for each pleat.*

3 *Next, measure and mark the next space between pleats – without 5 cm (2 in) for the return – and then the next pleat. Continue across the blind until you reach the other side, where you finish as you started with a space between pleats plus 5 cm (2 in) for the return.*

4 *To provide guides for folding the pleats, measure and mark with another pin the centre spot between the first and second lines of pins.*

5 *Measure and mark the space between the third and fourth lines of pins in the same way and continue across the blind until you have measured and marked all of the pleats.*

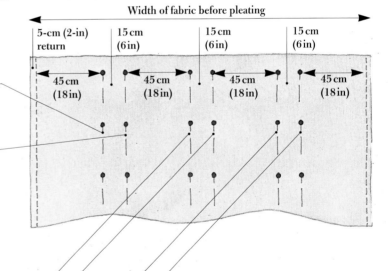

Width of fabric before pleating

| 5-cm (2-in) return | 15 cm (6 in) | 15 cm (6 in) | 15 cm (6 in) |

45 cm (18 in)   45 cm (18 in)   45 cm (18 in)   45 cm (18 in)

First line of pins   Second line of pins

6 *Starting with the first three lines of pins, fold the fabric so that the first line of pins meets the second line. Then fold in the other side so that the third line of pins also meets the second line. Press the folds in place and repeat for other pleats.*

7 *When you have pressed all the pleats, turn over the blind and check that all the pleats are straight and neatly pressed in place. Redo the process if necessary.*

8 *Turn the blind right side up and machine stitch along the top of the blind to secure the pleats in position. Make sure that you catch the lining.*

9 *Measure 5 cm (2 in) from the top of the blind and draw a pencil line across the blind on the lining side. Machine stitch across the top just above the line. This prevents the pleats from unfolding when the top of the blind is rolled around the lath.*

Cording the blind

1 *Position and stitch in place by hand the rows of rings up the back of the blind (see p. 54). Position the bottom ring 5 cm (2 in) from the bottom edge of the blind and then at approximately 15-cm (6-in) intervals. Have one row 10 cm (4 in) in from each side of the blind and one row running up the centre of each pleat.*

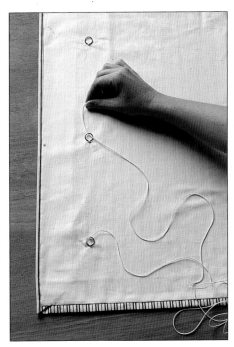

2 *Attach the lath to the top of the blind (see p. 56) and fit screw eyes (see p. 55), aligning them with the rows of rings below. Thread the cords through the rings, screw eyes and brass drop weight and secure them with a strong knot (see p. 54). You can now hang the blind (see p. 57).*

VARIATION FOR LINED AND PLEATED BLIND

The fringe on this blind adds decoration and texture and accentuates the series of scoops along the base. The colour of the fringe harmonises with the fabric used for the blind and so is in keeping with the simplicity of the blind's style.

FABRIC CARE

To make your curtains and blinds last longer and look better, you should handle them as little as possible. Most fabrics will fade eventually, but you can delay the process by always drawing them back or up during the day unless, such as with sheer curtains, they are specifically designed to remain drawn or down.

Cleaning

Always follow the manufacturer's recommendations when cleaning fabrics. Dry cleaning is the best option for blinds and all but the simplest of curtains and, if possible, you should get them cleaned professionally rather than using proprietary sprays. Some companies will come and clean curtains and blinds on site and re-hang them for you.

You can wash simple, unlined curtains, but remember that many fabrics will shrink, especially those made from natural fibres. Check whether the fabric is pre-shrunk (if in doubt you can wash and iron the fabric before making the curtains) and make sure you leave an adequate hem that can be let down if necessary.

Never wash interlined curtains and only wash lined curtains when the lining is detachable. The lining fabric and main fabric may shrink by different amounts and the curtains lose body and finish.

Only wash blinds if the fabric is pre-shrunk and you are certain it will not shrink any more. Remove any brass rings, cording and dowel rods first.

Dealing with Stains

You may be able to deal with any small stains on the spot. Blot away as much of the stain as possible and use a proprietary stain remover. Test it first on an unobtrusive corner of fabric. Avoid using water on silk or wool as it can cause discolouration and shrinkage.

GLOSSARY

Architrave brackets: slim brackets, usually made of brass, fitted to the wall or window frame and used to support a pole.

Blackout lining: a special lining which blocks out all light. It is made of a layer of opaque material between two layers of fabric (see p. 32).

Box pleats: a hand-sewn heading of flat pleats made at the front of a curtain (see p. 51).

Bradawl: a pointed tool used for making holes for screw eyes in a wooden lath.

Brocade: a heavy fabric, woven to create raised patterns and including some gold or silver thread. It was traditionally made in silk, but modern brocades are also available in cotton.

Buckram: stiffened fabric used to give shape to pleated headings. Fusible buckram can be sealed to the fabric by the heat of an iron.

Café clip: decorative clip that grips the top of a curtain or blind and encircles a pole support.

Calico: a raw unbleached cotton fabric with a plain weave (see p. 32).

Chenille: a soft fabric made from fluffy cotton yarn (see p. 33).

Chintz: a fabric usually made from cotton and generally printed with floral patterns on a cream or light ground (see p. 35).

Cleat: metal hook fixed to one side of a window and used to secure the cords of a blind when it is pulled up.

Cording: a system of cords threaded through rings fitted to the back of a blind so that it can be raised and lowered.

Cut drop: the finished drop of a curtain or blind plus allowances for hems and headings.

Cut width: the finished width of a curtain or blind plus allowances for seams and fullness for the heading.

Damask: a woven fabric with a special weave that produces a raised pattern and flat background (see pp. 33–35). Damask is made in different fibres, such as wool, silk and cotton.

Dowel rod: a slender wooden rod that is inserted into fabric pockets at the back of a blind, such as the Roman blind (see p. 96), enabling it to be pulled up in neat folds.

Drop weight: a holder made of brass or wood into which the cords of a blind are threaded.

Eyelets: a two-part metal ring used as a heading for curtains or blinds. A punch and dye set punches a hole in the fabric and fits the two parts of the eyelet, one on each side of the fabric.

Finial: decorative end pieces fitted to a pole (see p. 16) to provide a visual finishing touch and to keep the rings on the pole.

Finished drop: the length of a curtain or blind once it is made and hung.

Finished drop line: the point that marks the finished length of a curtain or blind.

Finished width: the width of the area a curtain or blind is to cover. The curtain or blind should make this width once it is pleated or gathered.

French pleats: also known as pencil pleats, this heading is made up of groups of three slim pleats spaced across the curtain. The pleats can be made with special heading tape but look better if hand-sewn (see p. 50).

Gingham: a simple, checked fabric made of cotton.

Goblet pleats: a hand-sewn heading made of rounded pleats that are stuffed with wadding so they keep their shape (see p. 51).

Heading: the finish at the top of a curtain or blind. Headings range from simple gathered headings made with tape to more complex pleated headings (see pp. 18–19).

Herringbone: fabric with a diagonally patterned weave (see p. 33).

Hessian: an open-weave, rough-textured fabric made of fibre from the jute plant (see p. 33).

Interlining: a combed cotton fabric placed between the main fabric of a curtain or blind and the lining to provide insulation and body.

Lath: a piece of timber, usually 5 x 2 cm (2 x 1 in), to which the top of a blind is fitted. The lath is then attached to the wall, ceiling or window frame.

Lath and fascia: a structure fitted in front of a curtain track to conceal it. The lath is fitted at right angles to the wall and the fascia fitted to the front of it. Track is fitted to the underside of the lath and is concealed by the fascia (see p. 15). The lath and fascia are generally covered in the same fabric as the curtains.

Lining: a cotton fabric used to back curtains and blinds (see p. 32).

Mitring: a technique used to make a neat, flat corner where the side hem and base hem of a curtain or blind meet (see p. 46).

Muslin: a fine, translucent cotton. Most muslin is plain but some have a white printed design to add texture (see p. 33).

Pelmet: a panel, made of wood or fabric stiffener and covered with fabric, that hides the top of a curtain. The pelmet is fixed to a wooden support fixed above the curtain track.

Pencil pleats: see French pleats.

Piping: a neat, practical finish for the edges of curtains and blinds made from strips of fabric cut on the bias (diagonally across the fabric) and stitched around lengths of cord.

Poplin: a light, cotton fabric with a corded surface made by using thicker weft threads than warp threads.

Punch and dye set: see Eyelets.

Recess window: a window that is set back into the wall, so that you can hang a curtain or blind inside the recess instead of on the wall.

Return: the part of a curtain or blind that goes around the end of a track or lath.

Self-pelmet: fabric at the top of a curtain which is folded and stitched to look like a separate section.

Selvedge: the tightly woven edges of a width of fabric.

Slot heading: a simple sleeve of fabric stitched at the top of a curtain or blind into which you slide a slim pole as a support (see p. 48).

Support: a device such as a pole, track or lath from which a curtain or blind hangs. It can be attached outside, on or within the frame.

Tapestry: a heavy, machine-woven fabric that imitates the look of traditional hand-woven tapestries (see p. 34).

Thermal lining: cotton lining fabric that is coated with a layer of aluminium on one side for insulation.

Tieback: a device made of fabric, rope, ribbon or other material used to tie a curtain back.

Toile de Jouy: a cotton fabric originally made in the French town of Jouy and printed with scenes of country life.

Voile: a white, semi-transparent fabric made of silk or cotton.

Wadding: a fluffy, fibrous material used to stuff goblet pleats (see p. 51).

Warp threads: the threads of a fabric that travel up and down.

Weft threads: the threads of a fabric that travel from side to side.

Weights: round metal discs that are placed in the hems of curtains to help them hang better.

Width of fabric: the width of the fabric as purchased. Most furnishing fabric comes in widths of 140 cm (54 in) or 120 cm (48 in). Generally, the width of fabric you use is less than the cut width of your curtain or blind and so you need to buy more than one width and join them together.

INDEX

ACKNOWLEDGEMENTS

There are many who supplied or lent their products or services during the making of this book. The publisher and author would like to thank those listed right for their invaluable support.

Jacqui Badham and Caroline Badham
Paine & Co
Kate and Paul Turner

Fabrics and trimmings

Abbott & Boyd
Bennison Fabrics
Designers Guild
Hodsoll Mckenzie
Ian Mankin
Ian Sanderson
Isle Mill
Nobilis Fontan
Osborne & Little
Percheron
Pierre Frey (UK) Ltd
Ramm Son & Crocker
Watts & Co
Zoffany

Poles and accessories

Byron & Byron
Mckinney & Co

Furniture and furnishings

Castle Gibson
Crucial Trading
D A Binder
David Champion
Josephine Ryan

Flooring

Crucial Trading
Fired Earth
Lassco
Sinclair Till

Lights

Sitch & Co

The publisher and author would also like to thank the following sources for their kind permission to reproduce the photographs listed right.

Ianthe Ruthven 14 left, 23 top, 63 bottom.

Elizabeth Whiting and Associates

June Buck: 27 top right.
Michael Dunne: 117 bottom.
Brian Harrison: 89 bottom right (des: David Rone Allan).
Andreas von Einsiedel: 15 left (des: Jo Robinson).
123 bottom.

International Interiors

Paul Ryan: 20 top (des: Jan des Bouvrie), 26 top (des: Pet Boon)

Marie Claire Maison

Gille de Chabaneix: 22 top (styl: Daniel Rozensztroch).
Nicholas Tosi: 95 bottom right (styl: Julie Borgeaud).

Robert Harding Picture Library

IPC Magazines/Jan Baldwin: 111 bottom.
Chris Drake: 19 top
Gavin Kingcome: 17 top right.
Polly Wreford: 13 top right, 15 top.

The Interior Archive

Tim Beddow: 18 top (des: Dido Farrell).
Tim Clinch: 30 top (des: Nacho James).
Fritz von der Schulenberg:
14 (des: Emily Todhunter),
21 top (des: Christophe Gollut),
24 top (des: Alidad), 25 top,
28 top (des: Christophe Gollut),
67 bottom left and right,
73 bottom (des: Kath Kidston),
95 bottom left (des: Mimmi O'Connell).